AF583865

a time of living graciously

REFLECTIONS ON GROWING OLDER

First published 2026 by
FREMANTLE PRESS

Fremantle Press Inc. trading as Fremantle Press
PO Box 158, North Fremantle, Western Australia, 6159
fremantlepress.com.au

Cover artwork and endpapers by Ruth de Vos,
A Local Bushwalk, ruthdevos.com
Printed by Leo Paper Products Ltd. Guangdong, China.

A catalogue record for this book is available from the National Library of Australia

ISBN 9781760995133 (hardback)
ISBN 9781760995140 (ebook)

Department of Local Government, Sport and Cultural Industries

Fremantle Press is supported by the State Government through the Department of Local Government, Sport and Cultural Industries.

Fremantle Press respectfully acknowledges the Whadjuk people of the Noongar nation as the Traditional Owners and Custodians of the land where we work in Walyalup.

a time of living graciously

REFLECTIONS ON GROWING OLDER

BRIGID LOWRY

This dizzy, scandalous world of ceaseless change.

—Rebecca Bradshaw

I dedicate this book to the young, the old, and the undecided.

And to Amber McWilliams,
who never got the chance to grow old.

CONTENTS

A BEGINNING

It has been said by some famous dude that the biggest mystery is that we don't think we are going to die. The other mystery, entangled with the first, is that we don't think that we are going to get old either. We know it, of course, theoretically. Then, little by little it begins to happen.

Our body starts gradually, or not so gradually, decaying. Our hair goes grey. Our sight and our hearing begin to fade. We go to more funerals. We contemplate our own funeral, a surreal imagined event that we shan't be attending in our current form. We read about someone described as elderly in the newspaper and think: yikes, I'm older than them. Once it was easy to get up off the floor, now it is not. As one friend said, it's like a Mack truck bearing down; or, as another remarked, here it is, our time of general decrepitude.

So, old and getting older, like it or not.

The next bit is equally shocking.

Death. For sure. For real. Zen teacher David Radin puts it so beautifully: *Each one of us will one day experience a day that has no tomorrow.*

Do we like it, the truth of our own ageing and the nearing of our death? Mainly, we do not. We ignore it. We joke about it. We may pretend acceptance but underneath, for most of us, lies a curious mixture of fear, anxiety, and the vulnerability of the unknown.

Personally, I was hoping to have it more sorted by now. I was hoping to have come to terms with my hair, my restlessness, and my anxiety. I'd planned to learn Spanish and spend more time in Samoa.

I've done none of the above and my time is running out.

Although if I live to the same age as my grandmother, who died when she was 101, I'm going to be old for a very long time. This does not appeal. Already my knee is so sore that the idea of surgery has begun to sound attractive.

I'm twice divorced, with no sign of my imaginary soulmate, the funny one who's interested in what interests me: Buddhism, food, and people, in no particular order. So it's not old age I am facing but doing it alone. Again, yikes!

And how will it be, dying? I don't want to be like the woman in the first episode of *Six Feet Under* who eats her dinner alone while doing a crossword, then chokes to death and isn't found for a very long time. I'd prefer to be the person who slips away peacefully in my sleep, sometime in the future, while still in command of my faculties. Or if not, to have an elegant not-terrifically-painful disease that gives me time to say goodbye to my beloveds and find good homes for my possessions.

When I drive past a cemetery I wonder how long until my turn, and please can I have the slip-away-peacefully-in-the-night option, not one of the scarier ones involving agony or a loss of dignity.

Furthermore, will my son remember where I told him to put my ashes? Also, do I want ashes? Might it be best to be wrapped in an old blanket and left to decay in a mix of sawdust and mushroom fibre, a more ecological way to dispose of a body. And where did I put the article that told me all about it and is it even possible to have a natural burial in the state where I live.

Here I am in my house that smells of toast and incense and things I forgot to do, writing about ageing and death. I could have picked an easier topic, but the more I contemplate this one, the more interesting it becomes, so I have begun an exploration that belongs to all of us, one way or another. Would you care to join me?

BEING HERE NOW

Young people have young people suffering. Middle-aged people have middle-aged suffering. Old people have old people suffering. – Ajahn Brahm

Living in this moment. Sounds easy, but let's not pretend. To stay present is very simple but it is also very hard. As Buddhist teacher Ajahn Brahm reminds us, we all have issues to deal with.

Even though the past and the future are truly non-existent, we like to inhabit them anyway. The Buddha called it monkey mind. Our thoughts swing endlessly in all directions. We lurch backwards, regretting how we messed up our marriages or said an idiotic thing last Tuesday. Then we fast-forward, fantasising about how we'd be happier living in Bali or going to Ikea to buy a flat-pack giraffe. Don't bother, they don't have any, and you don't need any more candles, kitchen gadgets or patterned rugs.

What is it that keeps us from being fully alive in the here and now?

Sometimes it's the present moment which is unpalatable, and can involve scary news items, losing our phone, getting a crappy haircut, or backing into a pole. It has been called Life with a Capital F, and it's like this for everyone, no matter how many pretty pictures they post on Instagram. So we run, hoping to escape feelings of anxiety, boredom, fear, shame, regret. We get lost in angst about the past, and fantasies about the future. We daydream, eat too much cheese, spend ages scrolling the screen or watching mindless rubbish—anything that provides some temporary release. It takes a great willingness to meet the here and now, just as it is, including all the bits we'd much rather not include.

Liberation comes from not excluding anything, including our own pain. The Burmese monk Sayadaw U Tejaniya advises us to not see something as a problem, just see it as it is.

It's important to find a way to peace and stillness in your own heart because the world will never settle down and dance to your command. Now is the only time and here is the only place we can learn to be less emotionally reactive to our own psychological content. To become less tangled in our own mess is a lifetime's work. Suffering is necessary until you realise it is unnecessary, as Eckhart Tolle says.

You may have to say to yourself a thousand times: *No big deal, me. There's no real drama worth the fuss*, but when the truth of this finally kicks in, it will be a wonderful thing.

Some days it will feel too hard, and you will be cross with yourself. You will stare aimlessly into the refrigerator, contemplate shaving your head or living under the bed for a while. At this point you can do what the monk Ajahn Brahm suggests and say to yourself softly, *It's okay, mind. I love you*, then eat a pear, go for a walk, and try again later.

YOUR STORY

At 33, I knew everything. At 69, I know something much more important. – Anne Lamott

When you are four you can be a fairy, a unicorn, a mermaid and an astronaut, all in one afternoon. When you're nine you crave pierced ears. When you're fourteen, you want to be your best friend, who is prettier. At seventeen you worry a lot about your hair. At thirty you hope you know what you are doing. When you're forty you realise your parents are getting old. At fifty you find some roads can no longer be taken. When you're sixty you might as well relax and be more wicked. At seventy you go to lots of medical appointments. I don't know much about eighty, ninety or a hundred yet.

Writing a life review can be full of surprises, even if you thought you knew your own story. It may bring up a range of old feelings and perhaps some new feelings. Take your time with it, or pour your heart onto the page all at once. There's no such thing as right. There's no such thing as wrong, either. Prepare to be amazed. Any genre is good. You can write lists, notes, poetry, reflections, dreams. An unsent letter is an interesting way to get something off your chest. It might feel good to write an encouraging letter to yourself at an earlier or older age. Write about your past, in as much detail as you choose. Write about your current life. Write a game plan for the next bit.

Here are some notes from my own jottings: living proof that you can have fun with it, and you don't have to get it right.

> Sandy-haired child hiding in books, reckless teenager looking for love in dangerous places. Attic girl in Sydney, with a tin full of weed and heartache. Buddha woman, living in the bush, making a baby, cooking for many, missing my homeland. Suddenly in a new marriage, middle-aged, mid-career, menopausal, doggedly doing my best. Living the dream, flying to festivals, almost famous. Once I lived for days on a baguette and fruit in a fancy hotel because the festival organisers didn't say we could order room service. Later I asked why not. The answer: in case the writers run up extravagant alcohol tabs. Oh, the mocktails I missed out on. At that festival I sat there with my books and only one kid came to my table. He had no idea who I was but asked me to sign his wooden fork, while the queue

for Shaun Tan snaked out of the building. I went to lunch. When I came back Shaun was still signing. Sometimes I like being a writer but not always.

I've done many things in my life. Some I regret, most I do not. I've travelled and had adventures. I have lived in two countries. I am a citizen of both, and like any migrant I can yearn for the other place wherever I am. Anything that happens next for me in this life is okay, because I have done pretty much everything that I set out to do. I'm a reasonable cook and a good teacher. I've had two decent marriages and quite a few lovers, some wonderful and some not. I have extraordinarily delightful grandchildren, a beautiful son, a range of interesting friends. I'm at peace with my wider family, whom I love and who love me. I despair for the planet sometimes and at other times I am hopeful, against all odds.

Sometimes I taste deep contentment, despite a lifetime journey with depression and melancholy. I am better, though not perfect, at resting. I've improved my capacity for self-compassion. My priority is my spiritual life.

If I only had a week to live, I would eat cheesecake for breakfast, smoke some hash for old times' sake, and ring every man who ever loved me and thank him.

You have seen a great deal of life. Why not write about it?

BODY

I was sorry to hear my name mentioned as one of the great authors because they have a sad habit of dying off. Chaucer is dead, so is Milton, so is Shakespeare, and I am not feeling very well myself. – Mark Twain

Here we are in a body, a place familiar and foreign, rich with delights and mysterious complaints. We have lived in it since the day we were born, yet it feels such a stranger nowadays.

We don't own our body. It's a rental. Sooner or later, we leave the premises. We can't control our body, demanding that it not get a headache, a disease, or broken limb, or wrinkles, or a troubling pain that may or may not prove to be fatal.

Many of us have a complicated relationship with our body. We've survived accidents, illnesses, eating disorders, addictions, pregnancy, or some combination of the above. We have felt too fat, too thin, too pimply, too freckly, too short, too tall, too something else. We have made babies, run marathons, spent time in hospital.

Now, a new problem. Unless we die young, we grow old, which entails learning to live in an old body.

Looking around me, the news is not good. Quite a few of my favourite people have died. Many of my male friends have prostate troubles, some serious. Three friends have Parkinson's, several have had breast cancer, some have diseases I haven't even heard of and the rest of us are worried about losing our marbles.

For myself, at present it's all about the knee. Arthritis apparently. Bloody sore at times. The doctor recommends exercise, painkillers and when it becomes crippling agony, a knee replacement. A friend reports that her knee replacement left her in pain and that after many months of physiotherapy, it still isn't great. Not wonderful for her, nor wonderful to hear. Surgery is more of a challenge for older people and is not always successful. Whoo-hoo, ho-hum and onwards.

I also have varicose veins and age spots, and I doubt you want to hear about my bladder. Every time I get an odd pain, I immediately think cancer, even when it's a sudden twinge in my toe.

As my friend Zoe commented: The ageing body, such a disappointment. Anne Lamott says her body has degenerated over time to grandma pudding—and aren't you glad you aren't Samuel Pepys, who in his last thirty years suffered badly with his sinuses, joints and bowels.

This is the way it is. Bodies decay and decline. Every person will have a unique combination of loss: sight, memory, hearing, hair, energy, body parts. You won't meet many who find it a welcome situation.

Let's start by relaxing. It's not your fault. It's not a personal failure. It's just the way it is. It is normal to age. It's also normal to have mixed feelings about our body, on the one hand eating butter from a teaspoon, on the other joining a gym.

Freaking out, pretending it isn't happening, or endless whingeing aren't useful. As long as you are still breathing, there is more right with you than wrong, no matter what else might be the matter, Jon Kabat-Zinn reminds us.

So look at the situation with kindness, get interested, treat getting older as the adventure it is. To deny the natural order of things—to reject the truth that bodies break down and eventually die—is to suffer.

I like how Ram Dass regarded it. His leg was old, veined, and bulgy. Initially he found it an unpleasant sight, evoking ego, shame, and disgust. Not wishing to be at war with himself, he reframed his response. If his leg were a twisted ancient tree, he would acknowledge its long courageous history, and regard it with reverence. In nature, perfection is not required. A flower, from bud to blossom to spent bloom, has its own authenticity. May we learn to hold ourselves with the same acceptance.

Despite not being young and beautiful, we can decide to trust the inevitable process of the body, doing the best we can with the way things are. Ross Bolleter Roshi suggested to me that we can cultivate equanimity and good grace as we play the hand we're dealt. Wise advice in general, and especially useful as we grow older.

Enduring sickness and decay won't necessarily be easy. Zen teacher David Radin noted that if you are heavily attached to your body and invested in it being a particular way, ageing will be more of a problem for you. This is a deep truth and worth pondering. It encourages me to consider my agency. Do I construct a narrative of complaint, or can I be fearless, despite vulnerability, poor hearing and annoying forgettery? Can I regard myself as a beloved mystery, not a failing machine?

At times we may feel a perpetual patient, days cluttered with tests and procedures. Recently I had a cervical smear test, a Covid booster, a shingles vaccine, a pneumonia vaccine, and I'm due for a breast scan and a blood test. I can see this continuing maintenance as a hassle, or I can have gratitude for the first-world medical system which keeps me in the best shape possible.

Each one of us can have confidence, for the body knows

how to do things: breathing, walking, sneezing, resting. We can provide massages, sunshine, swims, decent food, dancing, rest, hugs. We can aim for wellness, an equilibrium of body, mind and heart. We can balance looking after our health and accepting the reality of ageing. We can go to yoga, then relax on the couch.

As my mother said about almost everything, it could be worse. Rather than concentrating on what hurts and isn't functional, we can appreciate what's going right. In my own case, my main organs are functioning. I can play merrily with my grandchildren, although I'm not that flash on the trampoline. I can dance, and I enjoy long walks. Attitude is all. Complaining is an endless highway. It can't be overstated that the way we view our unavoidable ailments will either make our lives a lot easier or a whole lot harder.

Memory loss can be a worry but be nice to yourself. Losing the parsley does not mean you are losing your mind, and when you call the guy in the post office Aaron when his name is actually Jason he doesn't seem to mind.

Current research suggests we should do a bit more as we age, rather than a bit less. Find movement that you enjoy: walking, exploring nature, table tennis, tai chi, yoga, linedancing, cycling. Flexibility is important, and so is balance. Falling is a big setback so take care to walk mindfully down the stairs and stay well clear of people who text while zooming along on their e-scooters.

Mindfulness is also the key to managing pain. Adding fearful thoughts aggravates the situation. Recently I wrenched my knee. The sensations varied from a dull constant ache to strong throbbing. These sensations were unpleasant but bearable. The unnecessary extra suffering was the rapid onset of fearful thinking. *I can't cope, what if it gets worse?* I quietened the unhelpful voice of catastrophe and took a couple of analgesics. There was no real problem. If pain is an issue for you, do what needs to be done: applying heat or cold, taking medication, doing the exercises the physiotherapist suggests, anything practical advised by the doctor. Then do something generous for your body. Make it a soothing beverage. Apply creamy foot lotion. Lie down and rest. Listen to something wonderful.

As we get older, our body is not going to improve. It is destined to become fragile. The body is not us. It is a shell not of our own making, borrowed from heaven and earth, as poet Eiichi Enomoto so beautifully says in the poem 'Hermit Crab'. When we see age as a natural process, it frees us to enjoy the life we have.

LIVE THE WAY YOU WANT TO DIE

Sunday morning
I take my sardine omelette
back to bed
– Ross Bolleter

One day death will overcome its fear of trembling and take us. We don't know when it will be and, however much risk management we do, it will take us by surprise, one way or another. For now, there's not a huge percentage in worrying about it. It seems true that if you want to die with a smile on your face you have to live with a smile on your face.

How do we do this? Neal Allen, author of *Better Days: Tame Your Inner Critic*, says that our only real job is to wake up in the morning and be amazed.

Many of us have lost our amazement. We feel dulled or trapped by circumstance. We take the good stuff for granted. We rely on old habits and ways of behaving, trying to create a personal universe that feels safe and stable. We do this to protect ourselves from the truth, which is that every particle in the universe is in constant movement, everything will end including us and, in the meantime, things may not go exactly as we hope.

Our jurisdiction is limited. We can decide to eat a mandarin instead of an apple but we have no control over most of what's happening in the wider world. Wars, famine, climate crisis, inequality, homelessness—the list goes on forever and if we focus on these tragedies and the fact that we can do very little about them, we may well descend into despair, apathy, denial, addiction, anxiety, or just a general case of the heebie-jeebies.

Given this, what can we do to live with more happiness, more amazement?

We can practise gratitude. We can slow down enough to look at flowers, faces, buildings, paintings, trees.

We can do as much as we can to alleviate any social issue that concerns us. We can claim our agency. We can serve. We can help. We can put compassion into action, whether it is by weeding a nature reserve, writing to a politician, volunteering at a soup kitchen, reading to someone, taking the time to talk to a lonely neighbour, or any other thing that feels right to us.

We can aim for more presence. We can practise being in the moment, every moment, not just the easy ones. We can fully taste our lives, which are weird, and wonderful. Sounds simple, but it takes effort to remember to be here now, to not be lost in fantasy, in worry, in unhelpful thinking.

Never mind. This gives endless chances to return, to enjoy now, to tune in to the five senses, to soften the body, to pause, to relax. Staying in the body is extremely important. There is an integrity to it, a truth. Our body needs us to pay attention. It requires us to notice the tensions that build up and soften them, to rest when we are tired, to drink when we are thirsty, to eat good food.

We can recognise our feelings, especially the ones we have denied, such as fear, self-loathing, worry and grief.

We can practise excessive gentleness towards self and other. We can offer the world our gladness. The world needs as much gladness as it can get.

Zen teacher John Tarrant Roshi once told me that we must reconcile ourselves to our lives. This means to accept our personal predicament honestly and bravely. We live in a difficult world. There will always be strife, both political and personal. We have our sorrows. We have our joys. We have lost people along the way. We have stuffed up many times. We have become expert at avoiding our demons by changing location, drinking, drugs, living in fantasy, overeating, overshopping and blaming everyone else, to name just a few common manoeuvres.

Life will never deliver. My mother used to say that it was just one damn thing after another. Another way of putting this is that we all have twenty-seven problems and our twenty-eighth problem is that we don't want to have twenty-seven problems. Yet avoiding problems sends them underground where they lurk, surfacing when we least expect them to, or leaving us feeling only half alive. Authenticity lies in clearly knowing things as they are, including the uneasy parts: bad news at the doctor, grief at the state of the world, impatience while waiting on hold.

Stop trying to fix the experience. Just have it. Lower your standards and relax as it is, as Pema Chödrön advises. Accept that your continual search for somewhere better can never work out. Only by fully opening can we live our real lives.

Now you are free to appreciate the wonderful. Sleepiness. Ladybirds. Libraries. A child discovering their own abilities. Ice-cream. People who light up when they see you. People who light you up.

Enjoy your life. Live it without stint, as my Zen teacher encouraged me.

You've done the hard yards. This next bit is for you.

To live the way you want to die is to live with ease, gratitude, and a happy heart. Things will never be perfect, but they can be tasty. As my friend Irina used to say, after I'd recounted another tale of woe and drama, 'You will wake up in the morning and breakfast will still taste good.'

WRITING AND DEATH

And in my house what do I have? Only a bed piled high with books. – Han-shan

We are not separate from the world we live in, and many of our cultural beliefs about ageing and dying are firmly embedded in our novels, short stories, poetry, songs, theatre and films. Death and dying are extensive central recurring themes in poetry, fiction, and drama. It has always been so, from Ovid to Rumi, through Chaucer, Shakespeare, Dickens, all the way to Lynda La Plante.

Examining how death is treated in literature could be a topic for a PhD but it is interesting even just to take a glimpse at how writers, writing and death may influence us as we age. You may already have your own list of writers on this subject.

Literature sometimes provides socially relevant information about death. Many of the ideas we find are profound; at other times death is a mere plot twist, a convenient way to get rid of a baddie, or to reach the end.

Death can be the main theme of a novel, as exemplified

in the spate of YA books, TV shows and movies that tell heartwarming tales of a pair of young lovers, one of whom has terminal cancer. Although sentimental, these stories are popular, perhaps because they give us a chance to feel sad, as well as take comfort from a death that does not belong to us and feels constructed rather than real. A similar soothing view on ageing has become popular in the plethora of films for an older audience such as *The Best Exotic Marigold Hotel.*

A genre worth exploring is people writing about their own dying. It takes a special sort of courage and determination to face one's own mortality, as Dr Rodney Syme writes in his book *A Completed Life,* published posthumously. It also takes courage and honesty to write about death. This area is a wide field, but the books described below may provide a strong container for those of us facing our own mortality.

Dying: A Memoir by Cory Taylor is a potent autobiography, written in the year before Cory's death, while she struggled with a terminal illness. Shortlisted for the 2017 Stella Prize, this is a sad and wonderful book which speaks of courage, anger, vulnerability, and acceptance.

Then there is *The Unwinding of the Miracle: A Memoir of Life, Death and Everything That Comes After* by Julie Yip-Williams.

Yip-Williams died of cancer at forty-two. Her book

details her astounding life. Born blind, nearly euthanised as a baby, leaving Vietnam on a boat as a refugee, going to Harvard to become a corporate lawyer, marrying, having two daughters, then a terminal cancer diagnosis at thirty-seven. This story invites us to recognise the universal truth of death, and strongly encourages us to live our life fully and generously.

When Breath Becomes Air: What Makes Life Worth Living in the Face of Death is the story of Paul Kalanithi, a neurosurgeon at Stanford University who was diagnosed with terminal lung cancer in his mid-thirties. Kalanithi was enthusiastic about neuroscience and literature, and his career taught him much about living and dying. After his diagnosis, he tells his own story and shares his ideas on how to find meaning in our lives, and how to approach death with grace.

Peter Goldsworthy's book *The Cancer Finishing School* brings honesty, depth, humour, medical information, and a personal account to the growing body of illness memoirs, now known as autopathography. Both doctor and patient, he describes the intensity of his cancer experience and addresses what he calls the necessary narcissism of illness, creating a book that is rich, funny and profound.

It can be an expanding experience to share with others your favourite books or films about dying—and let a curated work help you find a way into having a conversation about this topic that people sometimes avoid. You may wish to ask your friends and family for their recommendations for books about living and dying.

My writer cousin, Sally Gillespie, said I should read Georgia Blain's *The Museum of Words,* which she describes as moving and real, and one of the best books she has read about dying. When I have, I know we will have a great conversation about it. Talking can deepen our own understanding, lighten the load and open doorways to depths otherwise unexplored.

There are books which take reflections about death and grief in new directions, such as *Grief is the Thing with Feathers* by Max Porter. Set in London, it tells the story of a man and his two young sons who are grieving the loss of their wife and mother. Along comes Crow: healer, babysitter, antagonist, trickster. It is a book both funny and wise, transcending borders by mixing poetry, philosophy, and magic realism.

Reading about death and dying serves a wide variety of functions. Recently I read a poem written by a woman whose brother had committed suicide, about lying on the bed with her sister-in-law while they laughed hysterically about the possible mad outfits they could wear at his funeral. Graveyard humour, yes, but also honest and authentic, reminding us that laughter can be helpful and healing in the face of tragedy.

Reading can offer spiritual and religious guidance as we face the mystery and subtleties of our own ageing. David Whyte, Stephen Levine, Anne Lamott, Rumi, Rainer Maria Rilke and Hafiz are some writers I value in this regard, as are the ancient Japanese poets, such as Han-shan, whose *Cold Mountain* poems invite me into loneliness, into the beauty to be found in ageing, and into facing the inevitability of death.

At its best, literature connects us with a wider humanity, offering a rich range of responses to our human predicament. As Kafka said, it brings an axe to the frozen sea within.

We forge our own relationship through the reflections that others have turned into art to share, and the wisdom they contain. Reading can encourage and amaze, deepen our appreciation of life and provide new ways of seeing. Literature reminds us that we value life dearly, that we do not know what comes next. It is a container for conversations about grief and for the deep emotions we feel when we lose those we love, and about our own voyage towards dying.

Film can serve the same function. Consider *Love Story*, *Field of Dreams* and *The Fault in Our Stars*. There are literally thousands of movies that deal with death and dying—it is the human experience, that we all share. The TV show *The Casketeers*, a documentary set in a Māori funeral parlour, is gripping, as is *Six Feet Under*.

Poetry and song can open our hearts to our deeper feelings which may be buried a long way down. 'Willin'' by Little Feat, 'Tennessee Whiskey' by Chris Stapleton and 'Glitter' by Benee are three of the songs I play when I need access to my feelings about loss.

However, let's not forget that death and dying are challenging topics. Sometimes immersing oneself in it can be a wise thing to do. At other times, it probably isn't. If reading or thinking about death and dying is dragging you down, it's better to walk amongst trees, eat cake, or play with a child. I have found this useful when writing this book. At a certain point, I want to be all about the living, and less about the dying.

CREATIVE PLAY

Every part of you is welcome here: your longings, your heartbreak, your flimsy dreams, your unique intelligence. Come on in. – B.L.

Playful creativity is a valuable tool to help navigate the glorious galaxy of your human psyche. There are many ways you can use creativity to help you navigate your own life. Here are just a few.

JOURNALS

I find them an excellent tool for creativity, reflection, insight and learning—as well as an important part of a wellbeing basket. Writing things down is a great way to work with difficult emotions. Sometimes it is hard to even recognise what's going on. Putting pen to paper helps bring things to light and is an interesting way to explore anything that we are struggling with. By writing it down, we give it some space.

CREATE SOMETHING

Bake. Mend old clothes in a funky way. Sew bunting with colourful fabric remnants. Embroider. Knit. Gather flowers, leaves and grasses, choose a vase and arrange them mindfully. Draw a mandala, a chair, a tree. Paint a wall, a landscape, a portrait. Choose something lovely that you no longer need, wrap it tenderly and give it as a gift. Collage a mood board of things that inspire you. Create a shrine to your favourite deity.

ACTUALLY PLAY

Play an instrument. (Badly is just fine.)

Do some dance moves with a child.

Cuddle your cat, or borrow a dog.

Visit a park and goof around.

Go to the ocean. Swim, jump and dive, do a lot of splashing. Stroll on the edge between land and sea, avoiding getting your clothes wet, or making sure you get your clothes wet.

Create a sandcastle, a sand person, a mandala made of shells, seaweed and rocks. Write a word in the damp sand, then draw a love heart around it.

Make a mobile using feathers, leaves, pinecones and other natural objects.

Sky gaze.

Explore new cuisines: vegan, Middle Eastern, Mexican.

Call a friend. Invite them to play chess, Scrabble, tennis, poker, but not all at the same time

Play with new ideas. Read about African poetry, Indian history, Stoicism, herbal medicine, mind mapping.

Find an oddly shaped piece of fruit or vegetable, turn it into a creature using toothpicks and buttons. Go on, you know you want to.

HAIR

Your hair is only 16% of your swag. Your personality is the other 84%. We make your 16% perfect.
– Sign in the window of an African hairdresser

Oh, how we all want to be perfect, to look perfect. As we age, we get to face the truth. We ain't perfect. Nothing is perfect and we don't look the way we want to. Hair is a good metaphor for this. Very little is in our control. It never was, but when we were younger it was easier to pretend that we had everything sorted.

Hair is a learning ground for me. I am the queen of hair neurotics. Ask any hairdresser I ever went to. I have so many hair stories. Five years old, sitting on the step in the sun with Robin, my pudding bowl sister. Away she went with blunt scissors. Fifteen years old, jumping into a hedge so my boyfriend, who was coming to meet me, wouldn't see my ghastly haircut. Thirty-five, a gone-wrong perm so dire my husband blurted out 'Jesus Christ!' when I walked in the door before he'd had time to think.

Our hair seems an integral expression of our vibe, asserting individuality, and independence. I have fond memories of my son Sam and his friend Leon, aged fourteen, cutting their own undercuts, dyeing their hair, creating their own style.

As we age, things change in the hair department. We lose hair in the places we'd like it and grow hair in places we don't want to. For men, hairy ears. For women, chin hairs! Another thing to come to terms with. Another opportunity to observe and let go of the suffering that comes from not getting what we want.

I've always had hair issues. It goes hand in hand with low self-esteem. When I have a hate-my-hair day, it indicates a self-loathing attack. A friend once told me she never wanted to hear anything about my effing hair again, after another of my endless sagas about it. She was sick of my desperate need for approval. Now it is up to me to reassure and approve of myself.

However, going grey is a challenge for many, including me. I coloured my hair for many years, to brighten my vibe. Sometimes I used henna, a messy business involving applying mud to the head and leaving it there for hours. If you were lucky, you ended up with radiant ruby-red hair. If you were unlucky, nasty bright orange. I also flirted with red tints: cherry, plum, mahogany. Brown hair was not enough for me. At a certain point, as I began to go grey, a tide mark grew between the dyed hair and the actual hair.

To me, this screamed sad older person. It was time to quit. An artist friend was dismayed. *Why be plain when you can be colourful*? Well, darling, because I am sick of pretending I am not growing old. The beauty industry makes billions of trillions of millions of dollars convincing people, mainly women, that the way we look is wrong. Don't get me started on wrinkle creams and botox.

Hair dyes are a toxic chemical mixture. They smell foul—and don't read the ingredients unless you want to meet ammonia and peroxide and a host of nasties with unpronounceable names. A number of studies have shown an increased risk of certain breast and ovarian cancers with long-term use of permanent dye. Carcinoma is a high price to pay.

Everyone must make their own decision about how they want to look when they are older. Sometimes it is not about how we look. When you undergo chemotherapy, you can lose your hair. At this point it's no longer about vanity, it's about life and death. Sometimes the new hair grows back differently. You might have chemo curls, or a new colour or texture, because the chemotherapy medications remain in the body, affecting the hair follicles.

I am not the only person to have had a lifetime of hair angst. Too curly, too straight, too red, not blonde enough, tra la la. I could start a club: The Unhappy Hair People. It's not just women who have to deal with hair changes. Two of my boyfriends when I was young had exceptionally cool hair. Drew was a Jackson Browne look-alike with long dark straight hair; Terry had golden angel curls. Now they are lovely older men. Balding lovely older men.

The real question is not about hair. It is whether we can accept the reality of ageing. This is an individual matter. Everyone decides for themselves what sort of image they want to project, what clothing choices make them happy. Everyone likes to be told they don't look their age. Intellectually, we know that we are older and that we look older. Yet somehow inside is a person who enjoys maintaining a youthful image just a little while longer.

The journey towards self-acceptance is a long one, as since childhood many of us have felt that we don't look right, that we don't measure up. It's now or never though. The more you accept and enjoy the way you look, the happier you will be.

MAKE A LIST

write myself down
on the back of an envelope
rye bread
tenderness
herbs olives hope

– B.L.

I have always been a list-maker. I've used them in books to create character, to describe society, to amuse the reader and to move a plot along. Lists can clarify thinking and elaborate possibilities. They can be poetic, funny, sensible, weird. They can turn into a poem or a plan for the rest of your life. I am a big list-maker in my daily life. I write lists so I remember to buy things: *bread, fetta, mandarins.* I write to-do lists for the next day: *vacuum, walk, ring the library.* I make lists of more important to-do's, things I need to do before Christmas, or maybe one day. Lists are a wonderful way to access your creativity, your spirit and your happiness.

If you are interested in list-making too, there are many ways to use lists creatively in writing and in life. Check out my book *Juicy Writing: Inspiration and Techniques for Young Writers* if you are interested in lists and their many uses.

So, get listing. Here's some ideas.

- Describe yourself, using a list.
- Write your life story as a list.
- Make a list of:
    - ◊ Great names for bands
    - ◊ People who once meant a lot
    - ◊ People you never wish to see again
    - ◊ Delightful things
    - ◊ Things adults should not say to children
    - ◊ Things to do while watching a sunset
    - ◊ Your helpful things

MY DEAD BELOVEDS—JEM

every night before I go to sleep
I invite all of my beloveds who have
died to join me around my bed to
sing with me
– John Roedel

It is good to remember our dead, to bring them to mind. Writing to our dead can be healing and help keep them close.

I met Jeremy in my twenties when I was at teachers college. Most of my friends were medical students who went on to become doctors and psychiatrists, which was unexpected because they were all loopy, and what we most liked to do was party. The early 70s was a fine time to frolic. We gave it our all in our paisley and velvet, glitter smudged on our cheeks. We smoked weed grown on someone's father's watermelon farm; we dropped high-grade acid from America, tripping out amongst trees or sometimes in the living room. Jeremy had a sharp eye for the zeitgeist. He discovered counterculture books like Ram Dass's *Be Here Now,* and the best music: Crosby, Stills, Nash & Young,

Steely Dan, Gram Parsons, Emmylou Harris. Jem was large, funny, kind and stylish. When he married Heather, also a doctor, they shifted to Melbourne to live in a snazzy house alive with art and music.

Jem became director of Adult Psychiatry at Monash University, training young doctors and working with hugely difficult mental-health patients. We lost touch for some years but later he heard one of my stories on the radio and tracked me down. It was a very tasty reconnect. I stayed with them when in Melbourne, and got to know their children, Zoe and Joe. My friend was still large, funny, kind and stylish.

I learnt of his illness whilst on a writing residency in Dunedin. I was living in a house that had belonged to a gay playwright. There was no landline, and I didn't have a cell phone, so I called him from a freezing-cold phone box.

Thought I was finally managing to lose weight, babe; *nah, it's colon cancer.*

I did not want it to be true, but it was true. Despite the highest level of health care, a year later Jeremy was dead. I will never forget you, dear friend. Two best memories. Helping you squeeze into black fishnets and a tight dress to go as Marilyn Monroe to a fancy-dress party. Sharing a bed at my sister's house in Mount Eden the night before I left to live in Sydney, not as lovers but as dear friends, talking the night away, snuggling to sleep against your strong warm body. Heather is still in the house, Zoe and Joe are adults now, and we all miss you like hell.

ACTUALLY GOING

When you are going to die, they say you are going to become Buddha. When it's time to sleep, just sleep; when you're sick, just be sick, when you're going to die, just die.
– Nanao Sakaki

So, death.

I am still forming my thoughts on this matter. I don't have all the answers. I haven't died yet.

I do know that I would like to give the gift of a courageous graceful death to my beloveds.

Coming to terms with dying is an exploration. We can create a tentative map, which may come in handy when it is our turn to leave.

Perhaps it is simple. Just wait until the time comes and then get on with it. When you're sad, just be sad. When you're dying, just die.

Possibly that idea doesn't really cut it for you. Everyone has their own relationship with their living and their dying.

For me, it seems a necessary part of my spiritual journey to give my death and my dying deep prior thought. Wise teachers remind us that each moment is a passing away—

a death of sorts—and each fresh moment is a rebirth, a fresh beginning. This seems an excellent way to think about it.

If we are all part of a great mystery, a coming together of particles that change all our lives and then vanish, where is the problem? We are here, in the midst of our vivid lives and one day it will be time to go. This is true for every living being. The noble truth is the impermanence of our individual stay. To fully understand this makes every moment we are here radiant and infinitely precious. Then our inevitable demise becomes a matter of dissolving into the great mystery, rather than a mistake or a personal tragedy.

My youngest granddaughter seems to have a good handle on dying. She's shown quite a bit of interest in the matter of death and asks many questions.

One day I enquire after her invisible friend, Hompah.

'He's dead,' she tells me.

'Oh. How did he die?'

'He stopped breathing,' she replies firmly, looking at me as if I were a nincompoop. What is it about dying that you don't understand, old granny?

Children are often curious about death. This particular child is very interested.

'Does it feel like when you bang your head on a rock in the sea and there is seaweed?' she asks her mother, several times. She then asks other things, such as how else you can die. This natural curiosity is a healthy thing which we may lose as we grow up, replacing it with anxiety, denial, and dread.

Most people say that what they're most afraid of is pain. However, even when pain is managed, it may be the unknown that terrifies. Relaxing around death helps remove some of the fear. Talking about it, reading about it, making it an acceptable part of an ongoing conversation, not making it a forbidden or terrifying topic.

There are ways we can get a little closer to the idea of dying in a positive and constructive manner. Writer Neal Allen said he learnt much by volunteering at a hospice, helping people write their memoirs at the end of their lives, and by spending precious time with his ageing dog and dying father.

Death is not the enemy. May we befriend the sweet, sad truth of it. May we accept the ambiguity and the inevitability, farewelling our family and friends with courage and honesty.

Then there's the nuts and bolts. It's very important to do the paperwork, sort out our power of attorney, will, and an advance care directive. Like many others, my interesting friend Steve has this on his to-do list. However, if he drops dead tomorrow, he will regret not having sorted it out earlier because it's hugely more difficult for those left behind if the paperwork has not been attended to.

These days there are a lot more choices regarding funerals and burials. There are eco-funerals and green burials, less monolithic companies and services available. Tender Funerals is one of them, a community not-for-profit organisation offering comprehensive information, holistic death care and support services around Australia. They help by informing you of all your options, supporting your right to choose how to say goodbye in your own meaningful way. They suggest you take your time when planning a funeral, and this seems like a good idea, especially if it is your own. Some people want a lot of involvement, some prefer to leave it to the family to take care of.

'You'll be gone, Mum. I get to choose the songs,' my son says, when I try to advise him on a funeral playlist. It makes me smile when he says this. I trust his choices.

I do wonder what will be said about me when I'm gone. I'd like to be recalled as creative, funny, interesting. I hope my letterbox offerings to friends, *New Yorker* cartoons and postcards in my untidy handwriting, will be fondly recalled. *She loved Van Morrison*, they might say, and *she was a good vegetarian cook*. I wonder if anyone will mention that once I was plump but later was thinnish, was once a pot smoker but later was not. Will they mention my traumatic childhood, my alcoholic parents, my neuroses, or will they focus on my devotion to Buddhism, to solitude, to my granddaughters? Say what you will. I won't be there to know or grumble.

There's sorrow in the human predicament, but also joy. However much we love this life, we can't stay forever. I defy anyone listening to Bob Dylan's song 'I Shall Be Released' to not feel a mixture of feelings. A profound part of understanding comes from allowing our feelings about this great and grave matter, including our reluctance to have feelings about it. On a world-weary day of small failures, we may be keen to go. This is where the phrase *shoot me now* comes in handy. However, on a day of delight, we look at the faces of our beloveds and to say goodbye seems hard, very hard.

I met a guy in a noodle bar once, a Kiwi who'd travelled widely. He spent six months of each year surfing in Bali, the other six doing data entry in Samoa. 'Places always taste particularly sweet just before you leave,' he told me.

May we find our lives worthwhile, right up until the end. May we hold this world with bountiful love. May we create our own farewell song. Such fragrant sadness, touching our deep longing, a necessary part of living and dying. For now, all of this for a short time only, as my Zen teacher says. All things arise and pass away in the spaciousness of the present moment. Even us. May Buddha and Jesus and all the angels bless your every step. May you breathe peacefully in every moment, including your last.

A LIST OF QUESTIONS ABOUT LIVING, AGEING AND DYING

Dying is no big deal. The least of us will manage that. Living is the trick. – Red Smith

You could choose to write down or think about an answer to one of these questions every day.

Or select some questions and talk them over with a friend.

- Are there any positive benefits to ageing?
- Are you scared of dying?
- Do you think there is an afterlife?
- What is the best thing about ageing?
- What is the worst thing about ageing?
- What does your body need today?
- What does your spirit/soul need today?
- Do you believe in bucket lists?
- What are some things you never want to do again?
- If you had a week to live, how would you use it?
- Is there anyone you would call?
- What do you regret?
- What do you not regret?

- Is there anyone you need to forgive?
- Is there anything you need to forgive yourself for?
- What is now gone forever?
- What is here right now?
- What is your most compelling fantasy narrative?
- Do you believe that you need something else to be happier?
- What would help you live more fully?
- What are you prepared to let go of?
- Given that you will die one day, what is of greatest importance to you?
- Describe the best moment of your life.
- Describe the worst moment of your life.
- Describe the saddest moment of your life.
- Describe the strangest moment of your life.
- Three things you have learned along the way.
- Something you are currently wrestling with.
- What is your ideal funeral?
- What would you like people to say at your memorial service?
- What would you like to be remembered for?
- Can you accept your past as perfect and complete?

GIVE THANKS

If the only prayer you said in your whole life was 'thank you', that would suffice.
– attributed to Meister Eckhart

As you grow older you can become more fully yourself, or someone grumpy whom you do not much like.

That's the task. It doesn't sound that hard, does it, to love the life we have. To be contented. To come to terms with things as they are, not as we'd prefer them to be. To truly love this life as it is, to accept ourselves just as we are. To be happy as it is.

As someone who gives it her best shot, I can vouch for it to be challenging. It's simple but not easy. It is a daily dance of dramas, devils, dilemmas and doubts, but in the end, it's the only game in town.

Luckily, you don't have to figure it all out. Best, in fact, to stop trying to figure it all out. Just meet each moment as cheerfully and wisely as you can.

Your ducks are not in a row. They were never in a row. They will never be in a row. One toppled over. One is paddling too fast. One got eaten by a turtle, and one flew away years ago. Just get through each day with as much presence and ease as you can, fostering a kind acceptance of reality and a sweet surrender to the way things are.

We cannot fix the broken moments, but we can have a heart big enough to hold them. We can use our kindest voice, wear our best scarf and zippy earrings, saving nothing for later. *One chance, one meeting*, as the Zen saying goes.

Don't hold back, nor be still waiting to start enjoying yourself. Now is the only time you have. One day your now will run out. This reconciliation with reality involves including sorrow, pain, loss, and all the less palatable stuff. To be okay with it all, to practise what Tara Brach calls radical acceptance, means to truly include everything. As my friend, writer Perle Besserman, says, trying to be present in the moment is especially hard when the moment makes unreasonable demands. Yet this too is Buddha.

Joyful enthusiasm can be cultivated. Friends and gurus can help us but, in the end, we must do the work ourselves. Appreciate this precious life, just at it is. There is no wiser option. How many times have we been told this by how many wise ones, but do we do it? Not always.

For me, gratitude is the key. Every day, especially on the hardest day. To be alive is a miracle. Most of my difficulties are first-world problems which I make up for myself. This is not to diminish the fact that living in an ageing body is a challenge, that pain is a challenge, or that melancholy is real, but when I put my arms around my foolishness, my failures and my fears, it brings ease. It brings freedom.

Here it is, my actual life, full of interesting things: a painting of a teacup, roasted tomatoes, dogs at the park, the shadow of a dragonfly, swans pecking away on the grass, their peculiar necks.

There is a commonly told story in which Zen master Sono taught a profound method of enlightenment. She advised everyone to say, many times a day, under every condition: *Thank you for everything. I have no complaint whatsoever.*

MY SISTER VANNA

Sober—
I bow with gratitude
To the moon

Bees in the basil—
she carries vegetables
in a fold of her dress

– John F. Turner

Here are some questions my sister Vanna chose to answer about living, ageing and dying.

What would be your ideal funeral?
It takes place in a hall, theatre or cinema. Mourners are shown an in-depth documentary of my life including photos, examples of my best illustration work and paintings, dramatisations of a couple of my stories, and the video of me at our Wade River bach reciting Denis Glover's poem 'The Magpies'. Meanwhile I've been privately cremated and ashes scattered to the four winds.

Describe the best moment of your life.
'We are going to be very good friends, you and I!' I promise, holding my day-old grandchild, Taylor, in my arms for the first time. Secondly, forty years of best moments enjoyed with my daughter, who gave me the wonderful gift of my grandson. He has given me the chance to become a better person.

Describe the worst moment of your life.
'Mum, I'm losing words,' Amber, my beloved daughter, told me one day. Words were her passion. For her to lose them was unthinkable. She was a writer who had just finished her PhD and begun her dream job teaching English at Auckland University. I could only hug her tightly. After struggling with treatment for three inoperable brain tumours, five years later she died.

Describe the strangest moment of your life.
Try as I might, months afterwards I cannot remember a single thing about the accident in which I was run over. It's a complete blank. Apparently, passers-by lifted the car off me so I could crawl out from underneath. I was able to answer the paramedics' questions as they injected me with fentanyl for concussion and a broken arm. I woke up in the hospital, the details of the actual event having been completely erased.

Describe the saddest moment of your life.
Leaving Bethany Hospital in April 1964 without my beautiful firstborn, who was crying loudly. I was inconsolable. I was a penniless art student and Wiri was to be adopted by a wealthy couple. My social worker, the hospital staff and my family all assured me that if I loved my son I would give him up so he would have a better start in life. Until the law change when he was twenty-two years old and we were able to reunite, we both suffered dreadfully from our loss. Since then, thank goodness, we have been very good friends, and he has kept in contact with his birth-father's family.

LOSS

alone –
her name rings
with bellbirds
– John F. Turner

We are all losing things, all the time. Not just that important piece of paper we put 'somewhere safe', which is always a mistake, but everything which has gone before and is no longer here, including our youth, dinosaurs, our twelve-year-old face, our grandparents, various memories, the ancient Roman civilisation, thoughts that once seemed important and now do not.

Mainly we are not in favour of loss. We are attached to the way things are, to people staying the same, to situations we enjoy lasting for a long time.

Impermanence isn't only what the Buddha happened to mention, it is borne out by physics: particles in all states of matter are in constant motion at atomic and subatomic levels due to their kinetic energy—a state also known as *everything changes*. Such a simple and valuable truth. Begrudging the fact that all things pass away can only bring misery.

Feelings that go along with loss range from mild annoyance to the deepest human grief. Grief is a valid response to loss, and we will all have our own way of dealing with it, but we can get stuck and sad for longer than we need to. Sometimes we must move on.

A parable from the time of the Buddha tells the story of a woman named Kisa Gotami, who became crazed with grief at the death of her only child, a baby son, and wandered the streets carrying his body, wailing, inconsolable. The villagers were unable to soothe her. Finally, an old man suggested she go and ask the Buddha for help. The mother pleaded with the Buddha to bring her son back to life.

I will, he told her, *but first you must bring me a white mustard seed from a house where no-one has died.*

The woman went around the village, knocking on each door and making her request. Each occupant was happy to give her a mustard seed, but they all recounted the death of an uncle, a mother, or another relative. At last, the woman saw the truth of mortality and was able to bury her child.

This teaching story reminds us that grief is universal. Understanding the inevitability of loss does not deny the personal but widens our understanding and softens the heart.

Loss is hardest when it involves the passing of someone we love, and grief is a profound and necessary response. It is supported in our culture, to some extent. When we lose a partner or a family member dies, people may offer kindness and food and more kindness. A grief counsellor can help us work through the complex layers of our feelings, but our grief is our own and we must find our own way with it.

Loss in broader terms can be more subtle, more nuanced. For example, a single older person may feel fleeting sorrow when they see a couple kissing in the park, because being young and having someone to kiss is no longer available to them. A parent may look at their growing child with love but also with a keen sense of bewilderment, wondering where their beloved toddler has gone.

Beyond the personal losses of our beloveds, there is loss and change on a vast cosmic scale. Douglas Penick points it out clearly. Without death there can be no life, he writes. The world we know is ageing and dying, falling beneath the hordes of the new. This applies to people as well as technology, political systems, music, cultural beliefs, anything you can name.

When we truly understand this, it brings clarity. It invites awe about the new and the real, replacing the futility of hanging on. An acceptance that things end means we can relax into the flow, the dance, the vibrancy of now.

What is happening is happening, whether we like it or not. Change will occur whether we like it or not. To accept this is to come to terms with the fundamental truth of being human. We can cultivate equanimity, a relaxed dignity not dependent on ideal conditions, accepting all weathers. We can hold the bright feathers of our grief and sorrows softly. We can co-operate with the universe, recognising the futility of doing otherwise. Otherwise, we will get rope burn. Ram Dass said you should take what comes down the pike, and work with it.

Now is all we have. Might as well enjoy it. I apologise for telling you this every five minutes. I tell myself, too, because we all seem to need reminding.

WHICH ONE OF US HAS DEMENTIA?

Yesterday is but today's memory, and tomorrow is today's dream. – Kahlil Gibran

Dementia is a fierce topic.

As we age, we come nearer to the existence of this cruel disease, its arrival in others and our dread of it. Some become carers for their ageing parents. Some become the person who has the condition. The rest of us live with the fear that we may be next.

Our fears are not unfounded. Apparently by eighty, one in four people will have dementia. By the age of ninety it is one in two.

This is a statistic I do not wish to know about.

Already I worry about my friends: the friend who regularly loses things, the one who suggests meeting up and says they will call but forgets to call. I'm sure they worry about me, especially when I start a train of thought that tails off with 'Where was I going with that?' Usually, I can pick up the thread, but not always. I am doing more forgetting than I used to, and my recall can be slow. It would be funny if it wasn't so unsettling.

For example, my purple outfits would benefit from a purple scarf, but I keep forgetting to buy one. Never mind, I can do without it. Then one day I move a floral scarf to see a lovely pale purple one beneath. My months-earlier op-shop purchase had completely slipped my mind.

It's disconcerting. It is as if there is a hole in my brain into which things vanish, the wardrobe door into a Narnia of forgettery. I try to remember a placename someone mentions. I recall that it's down south and contains N or P, but there's a frustrating blank where the word should be. A few days later, it manifests by magic while I am grocery shopping. Nannup.

Similarly, the flowers outside the library. I know *I know* the name of them except that right then I have forgotten the name of them. I know there are two flowers that are similar, and that this species is one of them. I know that in Auckland there is a public garden which showcases them, but what the hell are they? Later that day, the answer arrives. Azaleas and rhododendrons. In case you are interested, all azaleas are rhododendrons but not all rhododendrons are azaleas.

'I wonder why I keep losing my glasses?' I mumble, one grandmothering day. 'Because you're old,' the eldest granddaughter tells me firmly. Yes, child, you are correct.

Not all memory loss is dementia. It's normal for hair to whiten, hearing and eyesight to diminish, bones to become brittle, bladders and bowels to become less adequate. We accept these as a normal part of ageing, but we don't have the same frame of reference about memory loss. It takes us by surprise. Me? Surely not. We don't like it one little bit, nor understand it fully. Dealing with the lessening of our mental acuity is challenging and involves tricky feelings: shame, fear, vulnerability.

Amongst my stranger hobbies I enjoy visiting the Alzheimer's Association's website. It's reassuring. It lists normal age-related behaviours: forgetting a name, having trouble finding the right word, retracing your steps and wandering from room to room until you remember what on earth you were doing. It also gives you ten warning signs, none of which I am doing at this stage. Whew.

Our relationship with anything is the key, and this includes fear about memory loss. Many Buddhist teachers advise that we should not see something as a problem, but to see it as it is. It takes gentleness to see memory loss as the way it is, instead of making it into a huge problem by denying it or being down on ourself about it. I'm learning to cultivate an acceptance of my discomfort, both about friends not being as sharp as they once were, and the fact that I'm not either. To learn to be kind about one's own lessening abilities is an ongoing task and involves great tenderness.

I am seeing again and again that it isn't what happens, it's how I frame it. To demonstrate, I shall now recount a recent event in my life which I fondly refer to as *The Case of the Missing Earring.*

I always wear lovely earrings when I go to see my granddaughters. The youngest one often notices and comments on them. This day I chose a silvery pair in the shape of large teardrops, adorned with tiny blue sparkles. Late in the afternoon, after hours of creative play, I realise one is missing. I remove the other one, put it on the dining room table, then tuck it somewhere safe to take home.

That night I text my daughter-in-law, asking her to look out for the missing earring. She finds it the next morning at the foot of the child's bed. Hurrah indeed, except that now, of course, I can't find the other one. I search in every toy bag and art folder I brought home that day. I look in my handbag, twice. Okay, three times. But the missing earring is in the Land of Very Lost Things. It may or may not ever turn up. The interesting thing is that I don't really care about the earring. I have plenty of pairs. It wasn't expensive. It wasn't my favourite. The difficulty is my mind, and how much angst and energy I can feel about misplacing an earring. Instead of kindly saying, *Oh well, darling, never mind, these things happen,* I go over and over it, trying to figure it out. I don't like seeming foolish in the eyes of my daughter-in-law, or feeling elderly and idiotic, so I do some more worrying about memory loss and possible imminent dementia.

Even though I have written a book about loving kindness and can talk the talk until midnight, I have to give myself encouragement about how everyone loses stuff, that it will probably turn up at some stage, and that in the scale of things it is not worth worrying about. It doesn't mean I have dementia. It just means that I am no longer as crisp as I would like to be.

As my son often asks me: 'How long are you going to hold on to that one, Mum?'

The answer is: as long as it takes me to have enough insight and wisdom into the futility of giving myself a hard time. When this finally happens—oh, the peace and freedom.

PS I found the second earring. I can't remember where.

MY DEAD FRIENDS—ANGELA

woman's desire
deeply rooted –
the wild violets
– Chiyo-ni

It seemed a magical thing to have a friend born on the exact same day as me: 25th of March, 1953. Her name was Angela Middleton and we met, aged eight years old, at Normal Primary School, Auckland, New Zealand, The Universe, which we wrote neatly in the front of our exercise books.

Angela lived with her mother above a shop, which I thought was truly enviable, but an even more impressive thing was this. One day her pet duck waddled downstairs, snuck onto a bus and was found wandering around the Onehunga bus depot. There it was, a photo of my friend and her duck, on the front page of the Auckland Star!

Angela was sensible, kind, a bit bohemian and, best of all, she wanted to be my friend. A few years later she and her mother shifted down south, and we went our separate ways, keeping in touch sporadically.

My friend was impressive in her adult life. She lived for a while at the Jerusalem commune on the Wanganui River, led by James K. Baxter, which was an epic time and place in New Zealand history. She worked in photography, book publishing, retailing, silk-screen printing, social work and as the coordinator of the Ponsonby Community Centre. Later she gained an anthropology degree and became an archaeologist, doing groundbreaking work: excavating, researching and writing about the lives of Pakeha and Māori at early mission stations.

By now I was living in Australia but we met up for café conversations whenever we were both in the same place, usually Ponsonby. When I was on a writing residency in Dunedin, where she taught at Otago University, we had a great time together. Angela knew every op shop and café around, and showed much kindness to me, offering food and conversation in the funky old house she shared with her man. It remained a strong friendship, fifty years after we first met. Once, when Angela visited Perth, she managed to lure me into buying two brand new expensive dresses, which was completely out of character for me but not a mistake, as it turned out. We each had one son, and shared a strong sense of social justice, plus a love of the ridiculous. We called ourselves the twinnies.

Angela died at sixty-five, after a brief illness with motor

neurone disease. I knew she was sick but did not realise it was imminently terminal. It is a huge regret that I did not phone her to say goodbye.

We shared a birthday but my friend left the party too early. I am still here and she is not. Angela was earthy, fearless, humble, and a solid human being. One of the academic journals wrote an obituary calling her a bright archaeological light. She was also a bright human light.

Dear twinnie, it was such a pleasure to know you.

MY FRIEND STEVE (1)

I don't have a message. My life is my message.
– Gandhi

Here are the questions my friend Steve chose to answer about living, ageing and dying.

What would you like people to say at your memorial service?
This question suggests a unique opportunity for a final soliloquy. Perhaps we should afford everyone twenty minutes for their own final say. It would be a gracious way of wrapping things up for oneself, and could be something one did periodically, because one's insights might change over time. We will never know how it will be received so, as with most creative acts, the joy must be in the doing of it.

Are there any positive benefits to ageing?
For a meditator or a contemplative, this is a golden age. I'm also conscious that the wisdom of older people is not so much wasted on the young, but foisted on them, like a rich person telling someone poor that life is good.

Just today I was reflecting on the joys of being seventy. Your life is almost over but you get to relax and reflect on it all from a safe distance. I wouldn't want to be back in the maelstrom of my mid-forties. I made a lot of mistakes but am compassionate enough to realise that my younger self was trying his best to get through with faulty information and a busted compass. I am much happier now than I was at fifty, which was a particularly low point in my happiness journey, although I would not have realised that at the time. In my work, I have a fair number of older clients, so I get to watch as they grapple with the travails of ageing—some with great courage, others with dread and depression.

Are you scared of dying?
Yes and no. I like to think not, and that I will pass with serenity and grace, but I have some fear that I'll want to squeeze the last bit out of life and be forced to leave like an unwanted party guest. Naturally, the spectre of a messy and/or painful death is frightening. I tend not to think about it much.

Do you think there is an afterlife?
I don't know. I'm certainly open to the possibility but think it's a kind of vacuous question as we can't know. I like to think I'm an eager open-eyed explorer and will look

forward to whatever happens on the other side, so I'm hedging my bets.

What is the best thing about ageing?
After a lifetime of angst in the court of others' opinions, I largely don't care what other people think of me anymore. Secondly, the race has been run and there's no longer the weight of having to do things so that the rest of my life will be in the right order. No big prizes to be fought for, no great losses hanging over my head.

What is the worst thing about ageing?
The decaying body, as you are continually reminded of greater physical challenges and declining capacity. The further down the slippery slope you fall, the greater the effort you must make just to remain where you are. Sometimes I see this as life's punishment for those of us privileged enough to grow old. It seems that the price of life is eternal striving, and as life dwindles, the striving must get more vigorous.

What does your body need today?
Exercise, encouragement, warm baths, massages. Hot and cold immersions, and a range of supplements to keep me in better mental and physical health.

What does your spirit/soul need today?
Encouragement, affirmation, reassurance, friendly people, kind people, gratitude, relief from demands and details.

Do you believe in bucket lists?
No. Who would I show the list to? Who am I trying to impress? In any case the list would have been drawn up by a younger version of me and his appetite is not my current appetite, his wishes and concerns are not the ones I have now. So why would I let them dictate my actions now?

What are some things you never want to do again?
Obligatory meetups.

Looking after ageing parents.

Exams.

Coursework.

Finding a job.

Finding the right job.

Finding a partner.

Finding the right partner.

Finding a house.

Finding the right house.

Applying to get a home loan.

Trying to get a promotion at work.

Committee meetings.

Cocktail parties.

LETTING GO OF STUFF

light rain
on the radishes –
gone to seed.
– John F. Turner

At a certain time and age—different for everyone perhaps, but in my case, right now and over the past few years—you realise that you have too much stuff, you don't need any more stuff, and you'd like to get rid of quite a lot of stuff.

It becomes clear that you can't take it with you, and that it will be a burden for those left behind so maybe you should start getting rid of things now. As the saying goes, there are no pockets in a shroud.

When we are gone, a few of our possessions will be claimed and treasured by family and friends but most of it will not. My friend Mia calls this accumulation 'granny crap'.

Deciding what to keep and what to let go of can be dreary, fascinating, dutiful, a creative dance or a heady mixture of the above.

There's even a book about it, *The Gentle Art of Swedish Death Cleaning*, by Margareta Magnusson, an artist who says she's 'somewhere between eighty and one hundred'. (She's also written about ageing exuberantly, and her work has been made into a television show.) Her death-cleansing premise is that it's not only about decluttering but also about finding what's holding you back from letting go of things, and she suggests creative ways of finding a good home for something, rather than dumping it in landfill.

Finding the right place for things is an art form. Once I took six tiny wiping cloths, the ones they give you with new glasses, to the op shop where I volunteer. It sounds bonkers but I hate waste so I was going to put them in the maintenance shed, in case they were useful for wiping delicate items, but the shed was locked. When I told another volunteer about it, she took a wiper for herself and suggested I tuck one in with each pair of the old sunglasses in the shop. Problem solved, and satisfying to the point of joyous.

Generosity is a path to letting go. Giving a book to a friend or a dress to a neighbour who admired it feels great. Giving to op shops is sensible but only donate items that are clean and in good shape. Another way to find homes for unwanted items are online Buy Nothing groups, which are specific to your suburb. You can get rid of anything from a goldfish to a saxophone. Garage sales are fun. Do them by yourself or with friends and make a bit of cash. Similarly, holding stalls at trash-and-treasure markets. If your local council has them, verge collections are another way to offload unwanted items, from furniture to magazines to plants. Resolve may be needed so that you don't gather more than you have abandoned from other people's verges.

Sensible organisation is required when it comes to shedding possessions. If you list categories, you can attack each one by one, making the task less daunting.

- Papers. Which are necessary, which are not?
- Photographs. Keep some and give some to the people in them. Chuck some.
- Artworks. Sell, gift, donate, or keep.
- Clothes. Sort: too big, too small, just right.
- Linens. Be ruthless. How many pillowslips do you actually need?
- Books. Keep the beloveds. Pass on the rest. Give away, take to an op shop, put in a little book library, put near the footpath in a box with a FREE sign.
- Kitchenware. When did you last, or ever, use the egg slicer?

- Other categories: Furniture. Records/CDs. Sporting goods. Stationery. Musical instruments. Ornaments. Sewing gear. Craft supplies.
- Tiny things in drawers: string, bread tags, rubber bands.
- Things given to you that you never liked.
- Things given to you that you dearly love but are ready to pass on.
- Treasures you want with you right until the end.

Susan Moon, a writer and Zen student in her seventies, arranged to go about the process of uncluttering in preparation for death by doing it with friends. On Sunday afternoons, each in their own homes, they choose an area to be culled: sewing gear, kitchen items, old photographs, etc. They inform the others, then set to work. Later in the day they share progress, reporting what's been accomplished, how they feel about it, and anything else that seems important. An excellent and companionable way to avoid procrastination, for how many times does one say about decluttering 'I must do that', and then not do it?

It's not just possessions we can let go of. It's unnecessary ideas, expectations, an endless need to please, control or strive. Musician Josh Radnor says of the songs on his album *Eulogy* that each was a farewell to some part of himself that had served him for a time but was no longer necessary. He also found that the mercy of getting older was letting go of all those potential paths and no longer trying to live out every possibility. There is so much we can shed. We no longer need to be young, be successful, be anything at all, and at the moment of death, we can let go of everything. Some of us find letting go easy, for others it is harder.

Letting go means we can take our lives more lightly, cultivating a relaxed way of being. Perhaps this is what is meant by grace—to enjoy a simple life fully, after all our hard years. And no, you really don't need four veggie peelers, especially the broken one.

CATALOGUE

At death there will be much to let go of. Four Kuan Yin statues. Five Buddha statues. Two teapots: one serviceable, one decorative. Tea: nine varieties. A drawer full of tea towels. Four towels. Nineteen old journals. Twelve bras: some comfortable, some sexy, some neither comfortable nor sexy but expensive. I hoped they'd improve if I left them in the drawer long enough. All the books. All the clothes. All the shoes. Fifteen pairs of earrings. Nine frisky scarves. My beloved bone-carving necklace. All the houses ever lived in or owned. Every regret, every secret. Memories of past lovers: quite a few men, four women. Two ex-husbands. One adult child. Two granddaughters. Assorted furniture. Motley collection of art gear. Snorkel and mask. Photographs: India, Thailand, New York, Bali, Ruby Bay, Wade River. Words gathered and hoarded: blossom garnet ocean envelope hyacinth porridge pencil dragonfly. Any idea that life will get better soon. An unfinished piece of writing which says *Children are beginning to sleep in trees.*

MY DEAD GRANDMOTHER

Life unravels.
My grandmother
keeps knitting.
– Amber McWilliams

My grandmother died when she was one hundred and one. All her faculties were intact, except her eyesight. When she went blind, she could no longer live independently and went to live in a retirement home. Her friends were all dead, and the events offered, such as bingo, bus trips and getting your hair done, were of no interest to her. She couldn't go for walks or swim or paint, the activities she had loved. Her days were long. She listened to the radio, had a visitor on a Sunday perhaps, ate three meals, did not complain. It wasn't what you would wish for her, but she was stoic.

'I'm ready to go, you know, I'm ready to go,' she said, each time I visited from Australia. Her voice wasn't plaintive, just weary, and truthful. Then she would offer me something: an antique plate with a pansy on it, my grandfather's old leather workbag. She had no need for things anymore. Several years later she passed away.

My grandmother was brave and practical and forthright. During her lifetime she'd seen the invention of the motor car and watched the moon landing. She wasn't an outwardly warm person, but in her way she cared deeply. She'd lost her only son, Eric, after the war, a deep sorrow for her. Although wealthy, she lived very simply, ate sparingly, looked after friends from church.

She took me to my first theatre event, upstairs at the Civic Theatre in Auckland. I must have been about five. I remember red velvet curtains, a chorus of actors waving paper tulips. There wasn't much for a child to do at her place, but she did have a scrapbook of cartoons I could look at. I am not sure if I want to live as long as her but I live simply and have scrapbooks of cartoons about writers. I imagine she would be pleased.

THINGS I HAVE REALISED

No-one cares how I look. They're busy worrying about how they look.

There's no hurry. I can slow down and cross a few things off the list.

Resting is good. Kindness is good.

My friends deserve honesty and understanding.

If it's a first-world problem, I can let it go.

I am not too old to be playful.

Leave other people's business to them.

Seeking outside approval is an addiction.

Don't listen to your inner critic, Evil Betty. She's a total buzzkill.

Anxiety and shame are poor travelling companions.

Never try to cut your own hair.

MY FRIEND RO

Live all you can; it's a mistake not to.
– Henry James

Here are the answers my friend Ro chose to give when I asked her about living, ageing and dying.

What is your most compelling fantasy narrative?

Legs Like a Gazelle

When I was a kid I had a friend called Linda, whose sister was a marching girl. On Saturday mornings she strutted around in a snug-fitting jacket with gold epaulettes and a pleated tartan skirt. I coveted the outfit, but it was her legs I pined for: long and lean, with a painted-on tan that contrasted fabulously with the white calf-length boots.

My own short, stubby legs (now laced with varicose veins) have carried me faithfully and without complaint for over seventy years. But some foolish, ineradicable part of me clings to the irrational belief that life would have offered me more magic if only I'd wandered through it on the slender, tawny legs of a gazelle. Why, right this very moment, in my eighth decade of life, I could be strolling the boulevards of Paris on the arm of a dashing young Frenchman!

What do you regret?

My Greatest Regret

Out of a desperate need to escape my dysfunctional family, I left home when I was sixteen, in effect casting my mother and me into exile from each other. Lodged inside me is the terrible, useless regret that to save myself, I abandoned my poor, kind-hearted mother whose creativity and intelligence were stifled by deafness and an alcoholic husband. The true cruelty of my defection didn't truly sink in until I had a daughter of my own, but by then my mother was dead. Now I have a granddaughter who bears a haunting resemblance to my mother. If only I had been able to love my mother as freely and spontaneously as I love my granddaughter.

Do you believe in bucket lists?

I Hate Them!

I don't believe in Bucket Lists—especially when presented in glossy coffee-table books with titles like *101 Places to Visit Before You Die*. Life is more than a series of To-Do

Lists. And a Bucket List is just another bloody To-Do List disguised as uplift and inspiration.

What is the best thing about ageing?

Becoming Invisible

I know a woman of a certain age who claims—only half-jokingly—that she is now so perfectly invisible that even automatic doors fail to register her existence and no longer slide open obligingly at her approach. This isn't necessarily a bad thing. I'm inclined to think that invisibility is the older woman's superpower. It allows her to pass through the world unobserved, the watcher, not the watched. For me, and I suspect many other women, becoming invisible is a relief and a liberation.

Experience in Self-Management

When you are older, you're more alert to your neuroses and behavioural tics and therefore more able to circumvent them. In the past, when I was depressed, I sought relief in reckless displacement activity: getting a drastic new hairdo, running off with an unsuitable man or boarding a plane to Somewhere Else. In the far distant past I once managed all three at once. Experience, sometimes bitter, has taught me to sit with my discomforts and this is easier now that fevered hormones are not in charge of operations.

You Don't Have to Do So Much

When you're old it's too late to be an astronaut or a golf pro (if you ever had those ambitions) so you can kick back a bit—unless you have been persuaded to compile a Bucket List. People expect less of older people, and that means you can demand less of yourself too. This is huge relief if you've been an overconscientious people-pleaser like me. If you're lucky, you get a pension so you don't have to go to work every day. You get free bus rides, half-price seats at the movies and you're almost *expected* to go to bed early with a book.

Old Age Is Interesting!

All your life you're surrounded by old people—the grey-haired, the wrinkled, the halt and the lame, the bewitched and bewildered, the sufferers of invisible chronic pain, the wearers of hearing aids and glasses, the wielders of walking sticks and Zimmer frames.

Old is so familiar that you think you know what old *is*. But it turns out that you don't. It's a bit like a country which seems utterly familiar from books and documentaries, but which still shocks and surprises you when you actually arrive.

The transition into old age feels a bit like adolescence. Remember how baffling, intriguing, challenging and interesting that was? Old age is like that. Your body is changing. Your hormones are changing. New practical and existential questions must be answered. What should I do with the time I have left? What do I owe the world? What do I owe myself? How and where can I live when I am too frail, mentally or physically, to live the way I prefer?

What is your greatest fear?

Becoming a Crazy Old Lady

It's sometimes difficult not to succumb to the fear of a poor and lonely old age heralded by the loss of sustaining, lifelong friendships, a relentless rise in the cost of rent, power, and food, or the onset of disability and chronic pain. On a bad day, old age seems nothing but a disaster of ill health, infirmity and decline.

And what about mental disintegration? At what point will a lifelong tendency for non sequiturs and absent-mindedness segue into the pathology of Alzheimer's or dementia? Will I know when it's happening? When will I stop being me? What then?

What is here right now?

Moments in the Present Tense

I am grateful that I land 'in the present tense' more often

now that I am older, and it is one of the great pleasures of my life.

I am visited by the feeling surprisingly often when the dog and I go walking together. I might be in the middle of disgruntled thoughts about the mess I've seen on the way: a fast-food carton, an empty drink can, a supermarket bag and pages from a porn mag fluttering in the wind. And then some mental gear-change happens, and the separation between me, the dog and the rest of the world disappears. I am no longer a distinct and separate creature buffeted by storms of feeling—transient but no less powerful for that—of loneliness, fear, sadness, fury, hurt. Instead, everything, myself included, is miraculously imbued with this mysterious thing called 'life'.

EVERYDAY BUDDHA, THAT MEANS YOU, BABE

There it is again—
the soft gleam of happiness
at the kitchen sink.
– Amber McWilliams

I once told my Zen teacher I had three Kuan Yin statues on my altar.

'What about the Kuan Yin on the cushion?' he asked.

This is what Zen teachers do. They throw you an unsolvable question and then leave you to solve it. Kuan Yin is the pinnacle of mercy, compassion, kindness, and love. How can I be Kuan Yin?

It turns out to be quite an ordinary thing.

I talk about the ocean with the unusual boy on the Fremantle train.

I listen to friends' dramas, doing my best not to judge.

I stay in my body as much as I can, hearing the messages it provides.

I watch my thinking and when I find it to be completely unhelpful, I let it go.

I know when to turn off my phone, not turn on the television and do something quiet instead.

I tell my granddaughters stories about a giantess who eats broad beans and honey, who sleeps in a cabin by a pond and grows flowers that can talk. I invite them into the world of creativity, and in return they invite me.

'Let's be pirates. This is the ocean,' my youngest grandchild says, gesturing to the lawn. 'What's your pirate name?' she asks.

I tell them interesting things like how archaeologists have found the skull of an Ethiopian woman that is nearly four million years old, that there are over four hundred species of butterfly in Australia, about all the cuisines for which rice is the staple.

I try to show them that the main thing is to be kind and contented, and to live merrily as much as possible.

Kuan Yin with a teapot. Kuan Yin in the doorway. Kuan Yin in pyjamas. Kuan Yin drying the dishes, arranging flowers, wearing her dusky pink velvet coat.

AGEISM

decorated
tribal elders already
in brolga dance
– John F. Turner

Ageism is pervasive, invisible at times and very destructive.

An example. I'm at my local shops. A woman who looks to be in her late sixties walks towards me. She has short, bleached hair and is wearing high-heeled silver sandals and a short, tight, brightly patterned dress.

Mutton dressed as lamb. The words arrive in my head, unbidden and unwanted, a disparaging phrase my mother sometimes used, meaning that older women should not dress as younger women do. Intellectually I believe that any person of any age should wear what they goddamn well like but there it was, an instant negative judgemental reaction, lurking in my psyche.

We all assimilate ageist views and opinions. Being told you don't look seventy is flattering, but it also suggests that looking seventy is wrong, that looking younger is better. Phrases such as *70 is the new 50* also promote the idea that there is something the matter with being seventy. Family can be ageist, not realising how offensive it is. Seemingly innocent remarks can be thoughtless and disempowering, such as a brother's demeaning comment about his sister going grey, or the son surprised by his mother's Uber account.

Ageism is so commonly embedded in our language that often we don't even notice it. Calling someone an old codger or an old chook may sound innocent but it's a slur. We can all make better efforts to avoid using ageist terminology. Journalists would do well to write without age bias, and not reference age unless it's relevant and necessary. They could provide an actual age rather than calling someone elderly or senior. They could avoid generalisations, acknowledging that people of all ages have a wide range of interests and abilities. They could stop using clichéd phrases like *golden years* and *young at heart*, and instead call people *experienced, thoughtful,* or *optimistic*. Such language would support inclusivity and respect. Judi Dench says she doesn't like being called *vintage* and prefers *enthusiastic*. She also speaks of being older as a time of reinvention and great possibilities ahead.

Gary Martin, a newspaper columnist, wrote a piece about not using the word *old* for those over sixty, as it suggests worn out, broken or past one's use-by date. He finds *older* to have less of a harsh note, then offers some creative alternatives such as aged artisans, maturity mavericks, golden-aged gurus or prime-time players. His basic point is good: language should show respect and recognition of an older person's value and dignity.

Advertising is also ageist, so insidiously that we often don't question it. Being represented as dithery and doddery is as much a cliché as being positioned as a wealthy silver-haired retiree sipping champagne on the balcony of an expensive retirement complex. People of all ages can enjoy video games, dressing creatively, sexuality, taking up interesting hobbies—these are not limited to the young.

Then we come to our own lives, where we need to validate our existence, whatever our age, by encouraging ourselves to live beyond the clichés. We can adopt a firm stance, taking control of our right to be validated and respected.

In our speech we can avoid saying *senior moments, over the hill*, or *you can't teach an old dog new tricks,* or labelling someone a grumpy old man, or a kindly old biddy. We can refuse to surrender to stereotypes, such as that older people are hopeless at technology. If we internalise this idea, it lowers our confidence. Better to give technology our best shot, keep learning, ask for help when necessary, and remind ourselves that people of all ages struggle to keep up with the rapid pace of technological advances.

Anything that ameliorates the stigma of ageing is worth doing. Here's a creative response from a woman who, dismayed at the ugly institutional appearance of items her ninety-year-old mother needed, started a business designing and selling funky versions of handles, walkers, backrests, kitchen tools, perching stools, and other apparatuses. You can check it out at *grannygetsagrip.com*.

My friend Mia is a psychotherapist with a special interest in ageing and the psychological processes involved. She's on her own journey as a woman in her seventies and has been involved in encouraging individuals and groups to age in a way that fosters positivity and wellbeing. Mia defines ageing as a well-documented developmental process, and an important time of transition. As with any other new life stage, it has joys and challenges. One of the main challenges is the bias of ageism, which is intrinsic, invisible and limiting. If this natural aspect of our life journey isn't supported, our identity and our positive sense of self will suffer. Mia encourages clients to accept the vulnerability of this new time in life, to work through their fears and to live with verve and authenticity.

Don't allow ageism to hinder your mental health, sap your confidence and your enjoyment of life. Find your people, deal with your inner critic, go for what you want and need. It will help you live happy and live strong.

We are not only living longer but many of us are healthier longer, with good reserves of energy and zest. Our biological age can be lower than our chronological age. Many productive members of society are in their later decades. Frank Lloyd Wright completed a third of his work between the ages of eighty and ninety. I know of an eighty-five-year-old physiotherapist who practises her profession part-time, exercises diligently and drives her grandchild to high school in heavy traffic. Allan Jones is an eighty-one-year-old pharmacist at Perth Children's Hospital. He's worked there for forty-seven years, is still going strong, and is beloved by parents and staff. He was recently hailed a hero at the WA Health Excellence Awards.

We may have to accept the sheer indignity of being treated as unimportant by some but there are ways of responding. At a recent panel discussion, the inference was that all brilliant essayists were millennials. I spoke up, mentioning some famous older essayists.

Refute ageism. Cast it aside, along with the other bad isms: sexism, racism, sizeism and sadism. Remember that age does not matter, unless you are a cheese, and that age and cunning will triumph over youth and skill.

Ignore the billion-dollar industry selling anti-ageing snake oil, and rock on merrily.

Next time two young shop assistants chatter to each other while ignoring you, stroll up confidently and ask *Care to serve me, or shall I take this home for free?* It usually does the trick.

FUNNY HAPPY SILLY

The secret to living well and longer is to eat half, walk double, laugh triple and love without measure.
– Tibetan saying

The more decrepit you become, the more you need a robust sense of humour. An ability to see the absurdity of existence is of the greatest help as you age. Humour is funny when it refers to the truth of things, as in a *New Yorker* cartoon by Edward Koren, set at a sixtieth birthday party. A guest raises a toast: *Welcome to the decade of wisdom and more medical appointments than you ever dreamed of.*

I grin because yep, next week I'm going for a skin check and a blood test and I've recently had my pneumonia and shingles vaccines, things one did not even know about when one was a younger person. The cartoon helps me feel not so alone in my downward descent into decrepitude, as did another in the *New Yorker* where a guy asks Lost Property if any reading glasses had been handed in. On close examination, you see his glasses on his head.

As I wrote in *With Lots of Love from Georgia*, one of

my young adult novels, *you might as well laugh out loud because in 300 years your zits will not matter.*

Here is my current age-appropriate version. You might as well laugh out loud because in three hundred years nothing will matter, including your varicose veins, your purchase of yet another pair of tight shoes, or the fact that your friend forgot to text you back.

My friend Richard and I find humour in weird things, like car crash stories. I told him about backing into a pole while visiting the Buddhist nunnery, my mindfulness nowhere to be seen despite the holy vibe of the establishment. He matched it by telling me how he once damaged a hire car in Ireland—twice, once on either side of the vehicle. Such things are not funny at the time, but they make a good story afterwards.

In the same vein, at Christmas I always give my poet friend a book. This year I gave her a selection of writings from a Korean Zen master. It had beautiful illustrations, and, because it was not new, had a few loose pages at the front. I explained this to my friend, because we are eco-warrior women who do not subscribe to capitalism and we pass along treasures. She writes on my Christmas card, then goes to find a book to gift me.

As she hands me her choice, I say gently, 'I gave that one to you last year.' General mirth. Further amusement the next day when she phones to tell me that the book I gifted her fell to pieces. It's still readable though, she tells me.

Such events are best regarded as comic. In *Steppenwolf*, Hermann Hesse advised that we learn what is to be taken seriously and laugh at the rest. Benign amusement at our own foibles is an art worth cultivating because being dour is no fun at all. Instead, try gentle and kind and vaguely amused. Laughter is good medicine. Anne Lamott calls it 'carbonated holiness'. Buddhist monk Ajahn Brahm is internationally popular because of his unique talent to combine ancient wisdom with a keen ability to laugh at the foibles of the world and himself.

I can't say it often enough, both to myself and to you, dear reader, that we oversee our own mind state, and that contentment, merriment, acceptance, encouragement and good cheer are valuable commodities.

When I take life less seriously, I am happier. It doesn't take a genius to understand this intellectually, but it takes practice to know when to lighten up, when to try for silly instead of serious, when to see something as comic instead of tragic.

Most days bring something to smile about. The text I send to my nephew at Easter, saying *Jesus died for your sins, but not to worry, he'll be back tomorrow.* Silly perhaps, but it lifted both our spirits and was a fun way to connect.

Yesterday I ran into an acquaintance, older than me, a kind man who lives alone and once took pride in his appearance. These days he seems dreamier and slightly unkempt. I notice he hasn't shaved in a while and his shirt's stained. As I walk away, I look down and see a blob of ancient hummus on my trackpants. Tragic or funny—you decide.

Some lines you may enjoy from my lengthy internet research on ageing, from sage people unknown, which I conducted for the good of humanity:

It's probably my age that tricks people into thinking I'm an adult.

If you can't think of a word, just say, 'I forgot the English word for it'. That way people will think you're bilingual instead of an idiot.

It's never too late to be what you want to be. Unless you want to be younger, then you're screwed.

MY FRIEND STEVE (2)

Think of yourself as dead. You have lived your life.
Now take what's left and live it properly.
– Marcus Aurelius

Here are some more answers to questions about living, ageing and dying, by my friend Steve.

If you had a week to live, how would you use it?
Spend time with my partner, reassuring her. Make sure my paperwork is in order, so my assets end up at the right destination. Write a pithy living will to be read after I am gone. Arrange the playlist for whatever kind of service is to be arranged. Direct, as much as possible, details of how my body is to be disposed of. Help my family and partner so they're not burdened by choices and left wondering what I wanted. Get in a couple of good meditations focused on letting go and gratitude.

Is there anyone you would call?
No, not apart from my immediate family. Maybe send out a general forgiveness card so no one carries any guilt

for something they might have done to me. I'd probably include a line: *Please don't worry about anything you might have done or not done. I gave as good as I got.*

What do you regret?
Hmmm. So many things. Probably being too grasping in this life, too insecure, too competitive. Not being more generous and loving. Certainly, the appalling way I treated my father when I was a boy. The people I let down and disappointed at various points. Not being more tuned into my true calling earlier in my life. A whole mixed bag of things. I'll try and do better next time around if I get the chance.

What do you not regret?
I don't regret a lot of things I thought I might regret when I was younger, like not being rich and famous, having more social status, getting to a higher academic position, or leaving a legacy like a book or a bridge.

Is there anyone you need to forgive?
Not really but there are a bunch of people I need to ask forgiveness from, like my parents and a few girlfriends.

Is there anything you need to forgive yourself for?
Probably not being more gracious in life, not being more sensitive to the needs of others at certain points in my life.

What is now gone forever?
An academic career and all the associated aspirations. Big physical wishes like climbing mountains, going on long hikes, visiting famous cities, being a tourist, needing to have a fancy house, needing to have any particular material possessions.

What is here right now?
Love for my partner. Fellowship, serenity, humility, peace, gratitude, wellbeing, dreams, simple joys.

What is your most compelling fantasy narrative? Do you believe that you need something else to be happier?
I believe happiness is deep within. I don't really believe it's a function of external circumstances, beyond a basic level of sufficiency. However, I do have health anxieties and would be more satisfied if I had a stronger, more flexible body with sturdier bones. I still harbour a lurking fantasy narrative of living somewhere more exotic, the lure of *elsewhere*.

What would help you live more fully?
To be more loving to those close to me and, in an appropriate way, those not close to me. More contact with friends, more meditation, more opportunity to be with animals. I would love to have a feline companion again, but my mobile lifestyle doesn't lend itself to that for the time being.

What are you prepared to let go of?
Earning more money: not very holy, really, as I have held on to quite a stack. Needing to impress myself and other people.

Given that you will die one day, what is of greatest importance to you?
My relationship with my partner. Relationships with others, love, loyalty, being true to myself.

Describe the best moments of your life.
Feeling love from, and for, my partner. The birth of my son and enjoying special moments with him. Times which saw the fulfillment of my wishes: inner experiences in meditation, exciting experiences of joy, wonder and beauty.

Describe the worst moments of your life.
Divorce. My father's unexpected death.

Describe the saddest moments of your life.
Various. Letting people down was a theme.

Three things you have learned along the way:
It's all about the love you give and the love you get.

Loyalty is important and the most important thing is to be loyal to yourself and the people you love.

There is a beauty in being sensitive and showing compassion and if that's not acceptable to those around you, you are associating with the wrong people.

Something you are currently wrestling with.
Where to live. I have competing desires. Keep exploring and having adventures on one hand, the desire to be settled and not bothered with change on the other.

What would be your ideal funeral?
When I think of my funeral, the first thing is that I don't want it to be a burden, so letting people know what you want is a gift to them.

It would be a circle. There would be a meditation. There would be beautiful music. There would be my pithy statement about the inevitability of life and gratitude for my privileged life full of ideas and learning and meditation, and my wish for this kind of life to be accessible to many more people now and in the future. I would like a deep gratitude to my partner to be made manifest. I would like a flavour of simplicity, quiet, and sacredness. If I could request it from the grave I would ask for silence. I'd ask a commitment of at least an hour for those who wanted to be there. There would probably be some for whom this would not suit. I wouldn't want them to attend out of obligation, as it would defeat the purpose, so there could be an alternative for basic wellwishing and an exchange of condolences, as I realise this serves an important social function. I'd include the encouragement that here and now is an opportunity to reflect on the passage that we all take, inviting others to find the place of peace that they wish for as they approach the exit door.

What would you like to be remembered for?
Being a loving partner. Being friendly. Having a positive attitude. Being humble. Being able to love. Having a sense of humour.

Can you accept your past as perfect and complete?
Hmm. I couldn't say yes to that. I accept that my past was not perfect. I wish I had not hurt so many people. I can accept that it has happened and there's nothing I can do about it. I accept its imperfection.

COURAGE

It is difficult to find happiness within oneself, but it is impossible to find it anywhere else.
– Arthur Schopenhauer

I'm at my son's place, minding one dog, six hens, a large house, various houseplants, and a garden. It's a peaceful house, near the beach, with a giant TV. The dog is an easy companion and there is bounty: eggs, zucchini, tiny yellow tomatoes.

So, what's not to like?

Firstly, there's my dusty old shame. Author Neal Allen suggests we name our inner critic as a playful way of not letting it run our show. Today Evil Betty is meanly calling attention to my scrawny yet wobbly upper arms and the ropey varicose vein on my leg. She also feels I should be a much better person by now, without any personality flaws, or difficult feelings, ever.

Then there's the world, with its outrageous wars, horrible tragedies and scary climate change. A post-Christmas flat feeling is normal, but it's hard to feel entirely joyful with a wounded ego and a keen awareness of disaster (see above).

We are in it together, this messy realm of pleasure and pain. It takes great courage to face the challenges of our own lives, along with the vicissitudes of the wider human condition. We can find ourselves called upon to show strength which we're not able to muster. We don't feel brave. We feel sad, lost, overwhelmed, anxious, broken.

No amount of therapy, meditation or reading personal growth books will provide a life of constant ease. The world will continue to present its perplexing self. Each of us must find our own way to come to terms with this. Each of us must seek our own path to peace.

For myself, I aim for gratitude and good cheer but sometimes find myself mired in low mood, complaint and grumpiness. I forget to say kind things to myself, to remind myself that I have nice dresses, no major health issues, and that many people love me. I forget to buy treats: sushi for lunch, a bunch of chrysanthemums. I do one more weary chore instead of stopping to listen to the sunset birdsong.

Zen master Seng-ts'an said that true freedom is being without anxiety about imperfection, which is a great encouragement to accept life as it is but hard to do on days when the world seems completely screwed, and then you burn your toast.

Today I don't wish to write about ageing, life, death or planetary strife. I am world-weary, and sad about war, bushfires, and many other matters.

Surely climate change is not my fault—for I washed and recycled every gunky peanut butter jar my whole life. I gave up travelling for pleasure when I learned what it does to the environment. I stopped buying balloons and glitter. I took to the streets with my banner saying *SAVE THE WORLD FOR MY GRANDDAUGHTERS.*

What the hell?! I want to shout, but my oldest granddaughter doesn't like swearing so make that *what the heck.*

I will not write this book, I decide. My publisher mentioned the words 'solace', 'upbeat' and 'uplifting', which is too much to ask of cranky old me.

Then a ghastly realisation dawns. Whether I finish the book or not, I am still face to face with ageing and the matter of being human. There's nowhere to hide. I'm left with the wisdom of no escape, as Pema Chödrön suggests. Or as my granddaughter says: *Deal with it.*

I say a few bad words and keep on writing.

HOW TO STAY HEALTHY

This time, like all times, is a very good one,
if we know what to do with it.
– Ralph Waldo Emerson

We got away with all kinds of mischief in our earlier years without obvious ill effect, but we can't anymore. Now it's time to take responsibility for staying healthy and be accountable for the quality of our later years, doing our best to tend to our physical and psychological wellbeing. Ending up at the doctor with an array of problems we could have avoided is not the wisest plan. Similarly, ending up in hospital, or dead.

I have read a great many books on positive ageing, to save you the trouble, and this is what I have gleaned.

The most important decision you make will be to be in a good mood. Apparently, Voltaire said this and science is proving him right. Good cheer is incredibly important as we age. Recent research shows that having a positive attitude to getting old adds seven and a half years to our lives. How they got to that exact number beats me, but it makes sense. If you are thinking you don't want seven and a half years added to your life, you are probably someone who could benefit from adjusting your attitude. Smiley face!

Beyond a cheerful attitude, all the research leads in the same direction. Physical activity, good nutrition, community, connection, and a sense of purpose are the keys to positive ageing. This has been borne out by many studies, in particular those about the Blue Zones, places in the world with the happiest healthy old people, many of them centenarians.

Eating healthily is vital because it keeps our telomeres in good shape. What are telomeres? you may ask. Telomeres are repetitive DNA sequences at the end of chromosomes which protect genetic data and allow cells to divide. Imagine them as the plastic tips on shoelaces. Their function is to stop the chromosome ends from fraying and getting muddled. When cells divide, the telomeres get shorter, and ultimately become inactive, which has been associated with ageing, cancer and a higher risk of mortality. A recent study by Estelle Balan and others shows that telomere length is enhanced by the consumption of fruits, nuts, vegetables, seaweed, legumes, and dairy products, whereas it is inversely associated with consumption of sugar, red meat, processed meat and alcohol, so a plant-based diet is a wise choice for everyone, including older people. Eat enough but not too much and concentrate on eating wholesome nourishing foods. Have delicious treats sometimes, but chocolate, chips, pies and ice-cream should not be your staple diet. Current research advises older people to eat plenty of protein, so bring on eggs, peanut butter, and baked beans on toast.

Keep active. Exercise increases both physical and mental health in a variety of ways. It's apparently twice as effective as antidepressants for low mood. In New Zealand this is known as a 'green prescription', which medicos recommend before prescribing antidepressants. Resistance training strengthens muscles, which makes us less likely to fall. You can do this at a gym or at home with weights. The internet has many easy routines you can follow. Yoga, which combines postures, breathing, and relaxation, has therapeutic benefits for stress, anxiety and insomnia. Along with tai chi, it improves balance and mindfulness, which in turn lessen the likelihood of falls. Falling and bone breakage are two of the worst things that can happen to an ageing body. Anything we can do to maintain our own health and wellbeing is worth the investment of our time and energy. Another thing to avoid is being on too many medications, which leads to unhelpful side effects.

A new trend is cold water. Cold water has physical and psychological benefits. It improves immune responses. Also, it is fun. Fun is good. You can swim in the sea, finish your shower with a cold spritz or do icy bathing for instant reinvigoration. The Finns, who follow saunas with rolling in the snow, are onto something.

Your next wellness task sounds easy but is a practice, rather than an instant fix.

Learn to relax. Time spent worrying and being tense is wasted time. As Anne Lamott says, one superpower of being old is that you realise things are probably going to work out without your tense, controlling input. Learn to surrender, and trust in the good. Otherwise, you'll be pissed off and exhausted quite a bit of the time, and that's no way to live out whatever years you have left. Acute and chronic stress lead to cell inflammation, which in turn affects age-related conditions such as cancer, heart disease and memory loss. Find stress-busters that work for you, be it the gym or the beach, turning off your phone, talking to a friend, taking a nap or listening to music.

Try new things. The world is abundant with interesting activities so embark upon something new, such as joining an art class, a dance class, a choir, a men's shed or a book club. Not only will you meet new people, but doing new activities will help your brain create new neural pathways. Conscious ageing embraces change, and life is more interesting when we let go of rigidity and unstick from dull routines and old patterns of behaviour.

Another key to enjoying a vibrant older age is having a generous response to the world. Lewis Richmond speaks of four stages of growing older: acceptance, adaptation, appreciation and finally eldering, a time when we explore what we can give back and offer to others. Being a useful elder is a win-win because giving not only helps others, but it also brings meaning and purpose to our own life. There are so many ways to give back, and volunteering is a great place to start.

One great example of elder volunteering is an initiative in California matching retirees with underprivileged children and at-risk teenagers in order to lift their aspirations and opportunities. Volunteers are paid a stipend and spend fifteen hours a week making good things happen for the younger folk. This program increased the mental wellbeing of both generations.

Each of us has something to share. We all know about something, be it card games, cooking, sewing, gardening, first aid, photography, or kind listening. What are your skills? Maybe you would enjoy hearing kids read, mentoring a teenager, showing people around the art gallery, regenerating bush, helping at a food bank, running a workshop on vegan cooking or DIY. Let us find ways to take our love out into the world, as meditation teacher Vinny Ferraro suggests.

Finding a way to share your talents will help you to connect, which is excellent, because social interaction is a very important factor in positive ageing. If I may politely mention it, getting out and meeting new people is of great benefit, because some of our friends are going to die, so we will need a few new ones.

Lastly, take pleasure in small things. This is your life. These are your mornings and afternoons, your days and your nights. Now that most of the big events are over, like finding a job or a partner, or making babies, take the freedom and savour the quiet moments. A piece of music. The smell of sandalwood soap. The wink of a stranger as you wait in a queue. There's not much else, and this is everything.

Take Voltaire's advice seriously. The most important decision you make will be to be in a good mood. After that you only have to cease eating ice-cream for breakfast, take up volleyball, stick an ice cube down your trousers and teach someone to yodel, then all will be well.

AN ALPHABET OF GHOSTS

Zikhrono livrakha. (May his memory be a blessing.)
Zikhronah livrakha. (May her memory be a blessing.)
– Jewish honorific for the dead

I've lived in my retirement village for fourteen years. When someone dies their apartment is revamped, and a new person arrives. These are some of the people who once lived here but are no longer living. Their memories remain.

S.
Liked pretty things. Warm and friendly, in the main, but occasionally became snippy. I sometimes hear her voice in the corridor, except she is dead.

K.
Yorkshireman. Owned a huge library of dusty books. Wore shorts every day except on two occasions: when he went to the opera, and when he attended the AGM of the Youth Hostel Association. Had been a cartographer for the government. Took the train to Midland, where his office had been, once a year. Got off the train, said to himself that

he was glad he didn't work there anymore, got back on the train and came home.

G.
A good cook. He gave away dainty portions of Thai green curry if you were ill, or just because he liked you. A florist, he had lost the family fortune in mysterious circumstances. One afternoon he went to hospital with chest pains. They checked him out and sent him home. The next day there he was. In a chair near the door. Pale and peaceful, no longer breathing.

H.
Memory loss and a small dog. Varied from charming to barking. Both of them.

T.
Turned up at my door one festive season, very drunk, bearing a small Christmas pudding, and tried to kiss me. Previously lived with his mother. Enjoyed painting.

N.
Scottish. Soft and gentle. Flew back to Scotland each year to see her family until it got too hard. Became vaguer and vaguer. I inherited her damask curtains.

W.
Journalist, ad-man, sharp-witted. Passed *New Yorker*s on to me. Good on the craic. Alcohol and cigarettes were his best friends. Slowly drank himself to death.

E.
Very old. One hundred, in fact. Worked for an accountant, using a comptometer—the precursor to a calculator, now found only in museums. She often mentioned this. Her mind was sharp, her bladder no longer functional. Enjoyed a visitor if you brought something sweet and did not stay too long.

H.
Played the piano. Sat in the courtyard, waiting for gossip. Bright and likeable. Had done many things, including owning a banana plantation in Carnarvon.

J.
Ex-army. Quick to get irritable, especially with women. Had handyman skills, used them grudgingly.

P.
Friendly, kind. Artistic streak. Had lots of indoor plants. Really missed his wife.

F.
A mathematics teacher. Wore bright shirts and loved the Zydecats. His ex-wife and her new partner also live in our building. They all got on well.

J.
Upholsterer. Was unhappy to be here at first but gradually adjusted. Relished Friday night Happy Hours. Major health issues. Pneumonia finally took him out.

One day it will be my turn to be remembered:

B.
From New Zealand. Friendly. Liked scarves. Bit of a nut about recycling.

SPACIOUS PERSPECTIVE

The happiness of your life depends on the quality of your thoughts. – Marcus Aurelius

Some days you do your best and nothing goes right.

You go for your daily walk, because keeping active is what older persons are meant to do, and a stick scratches you through the top of your shoe.

You burn the blackberry crumble. You say a rude word, remove the scorched raisins from the top, douse it with cream and hope for the best. Disappointing.

Your hairdresser cuts one side of your bob perfectly but hacks out a weird gap over the other ear. He refuses to admit wrongdoing, tries his Belgium charm, suggests you come in every week, as the women in Europe do. You don't wish to pay him fifty dollars weekly to have him blow-dry your hair so that it disguises the problem he's pretending not to see. You must live with this troubling hair situation. Dithering ensues: continue to go to his salon, or hate him forever and find a new hairdresser.

And where on earth is the envelope with the cash in, that you put in a safe place and now cannot find?

First-world problems, yes, but on top of drought, bushfires, famine, wars, and chums with major health issues, it's a lot. Feelings of world-weariness, actual weariness and gloom arise.

A spacious view is helpful. Reminding yourself of the other eight billion people on this earth and what they are going through puts your problems into perspective. Winston Churchill's advice to KBO—*keep buggering on*—is handy, as is Turkish food, walking amongst trees, a bunch of flowers, a good book, an early night. Maybe the book mentions the Buddha's take on things. By golly, he was right. Life involves satisfactoriness, and this too will pass.

In my case, it took a matter of minutes until I was over the stick attack in the park. In an hour, I'd forgotten about my dodgy dessert, and in a few months my bad haircut will fade into the distance along with every other questionable haircut of my life.

The narratives we spin create our reality. Despite our challenges, from the mundane to the profound, it is possible to cultivate good cheer and equanimity, for our own sake and for the sake of those around us. We are our own responsibility and when we say yes to the whole catastrophe, it's a gift to ourselves and a gift to others. Camus said that in the depths of winter he finally learned that inside him was an unconquerable summer. This is encouraging.

It may seem counterintuitive but remembering that we're subject to ageing, sickness and death can free us up. My friend Sue says she can cut through any amount of bullshit by reminding herself not to get caught up because *you're only going to die.*

Shit definitely happens, though. Someone I know went to the doctor with a sore neck. Nothing much, she thought, but it was cancer, which had spread through her body and was now in her bones. Four painful months later she died. Fear loves to imagine worst-case scenarios but sometimes things turn out to be real worst-case scenarios, so fear and anxiety are understandable reactions to bodily ailments as we age. Our culture has taught us to fear death. Many of us also feel wrong about ageing, about our relationship to our failing bodies and the imminence of the fact that our time will come. It can all seem like failure and wrongness.

No point complaining, no-one's listening, as some wit said. Our options are to stay stuck in our difficult feelings or shift the energy.

It's a sunny day outside. Lift your vibe, girl. This was said to a struggling friend of mine. She didn't find it easy to hear but I think that when one is mired in one's own misery it's an idea worth considering. *We are our own commotion*, as Ross Bolleter Roshi told me.

It sounds so easy to suggest we can just lift our game, and if you are struggling with depression or any other poo-poo-bum-bum feelings, as one of my granddaughters calls them, you will be hating me at this point, but I feel qualified to speak about lifting one's vibe because it's my own necessary, daily task.

Without meaning to bum you out, here's my own story. I've struggled with melancholy my whole life and lived through two major depressive episodes. The first was in my twenties. I hadn't had any help with early family trauma and was taking lots of recreational drugs, a bad combination. I spent many months wafer-thin, almost totally silent and pretty nuts. The second episode came in my late fifties, after a sudden marriage break-up. It was a year from hell which I don't fully remember because I was hospitalised and medicated to the eyeballs, with a side order of relentless shock treatment. Since then, I've put huge effort into reclaiming my mental health, which can be fragile at times. I've come to terms with parts of my life and my character which I could no longer ignore, and I use the tools I recommend to you because they work for me. I hope they will have some value.

We all must find our own way. I've learned not to focus on the scary, the hard and the awful. Ivan Nuru's advice—

if it's out of your hands it deserves freedom from your mind as well—is gospel to me. I don't doomscroll or read huge amounts of detail about horrific catastrophes about which I can do nothing. I don't watch horror movies or shows with gratuitous violence. I don't get overly involved in political debate. I do whatever I can to help society, and I do whatever I can that helps me feel glad to be alive. When I tilt towards contentment and gratitude, I feel better. When I lean into creativity and amazement, I feel better. This serves as an offering to the world, which does not seem to benefit from my despair.

I'm keen to enjoy this last bit, to relish the ride with grace, merriment and ease. I encourage you to be faithful to your own experience, and to treat yourself with the most tender kindness imaginable, from now until forever.

may children wear hats, may birds speak poetry
may your soft body rest & your breakfast taste good

EPITAPHS

Ad astra per aspera—To the stars through difficulties
Vita brevis—Life is short
Memoria de valens vivat tamque vestri—Your memory lives on

Epitaphs are words written on a grave or tombstone in memory of the one buried there: *In Fond Memory. Forever Remembered*. They are sometimes included in eulogies, and/or in the funeral handout. Famous people have said fabulous things, and so have ordinary people. At the Père Lachaise cemetery in Paris you will see many famous dead people, and many famous epitaphs, including this one: *True to his own spirit*—Jim Morrison.

Composing your own epitaph is an interesting creative exercise. You might like to try this epitaph game.

Make a list of how you spend your time, for example:

- I am on my phone a lot.
- I interrupt people when they speak.
- I hurry and it is stressful.

Now make a list of how it will look on your epitaph:

- *He was on his phone a lot*
- *She interrupted people when they spoke*
- *She hurried and it was stressful*

Now write down what you would really like your epitaph to say. Mine might be:

Writer, mother, grandmother, auntie, kind friend. Buddhist, creative, brave. She loved to dance.

CEMETERIES

YALGOO

Old tins, old bones, old dreams,
dust wind, vast land and loneliness.

Many have died here, come and gone.
The cemetery verifies this,
glass domes over marble roses,
desert angels with gentle alabaster hands
clasped eternally in the ghost-town breeze.

So many stories rest here,
the cowboy struck by lightning,
the lost children, the Chinese gardener,
and your own halfwritten story
called into dusty focus
by the open invitation
of the neat, waiting hole.

There's a sweet sorrow to it all.
The wide, burnt, empty street,

watered rose in the hard dirt yard,
clear infinity of the desert night,
echo, memories, an ache in the heart.

A point all on its own,
somewhere far from anywhere
between highway and horizon.

Yalgoo, you're a landscape
and a beer bottle
and a small-town melody
to be played on pedal steel guitar
with old man wind howling descant.

– B.L.

Cemeteries are places of contemplation. How clear it becomes that everything vanishes, everyone dies. Mouldy vases, ruins of fake flowers stuck in the wire fence, marble angels, new bouquets. Walking amongst graves, walking amongst ghosts, walking in sunshine on a soft afternoon.

Writer Susan Moon finds cemetery strolling a profound way of touching the flow of time, a remembrance that we're all part of a turning over, generation after generation. Reading about the dead brings her alive to the fact of being only one person, not so important in the grand scheme of things. Like me, she finds cemeteries are a good place to have a think about things. They remind us of our aliveness and our mortality, of our place in the wider human family.

Some graves are well tended, some are long forgotten. Histories etched in stone, written in brief, composed by someone who cared for us.

We love you.
We miss you.
We will never forget you.

Words to say things that cannot be captured in words. We are all in it together. The couple who died within days of each other. A baby who lived only hours. The handsome young Italian father who left his wife and kids behind. The teenage boy, the middle-aged woman, a soldier in a war.

On a huge property in upstate New York, I came across the grave of a little boy, a family member of the benefactors of the sculpture park and writing residency.

For Alexander Jerome Willows Greenburger
May 27th, 1988 – August 19th, 1990

The long inscription reads, in part:

> *Before he died, he had learned to say I love you, please, thank you and I'm sorry. We remember his constant urgings that we 'read book'. He touched all who knew him. He was a perfect, magic boy. He died in the water, a place he loved. We remain on earth, in awe of his brief presence here, graced by the aura of his brief life. Our thoughts of him bring our greatest joy and our deepest sorrow.*

Such heartfelt heartbreak. One of the hardest things one could ever do is to bury one's child.

At the other end of the spectrum of human response, some people write funny epitaphs. Spike Milligan is famous for his inscription which reads, in Irish, *Dúirt mé leat go raibh mé breoite (I told you I was ill)*. How about the following, all real apparently:

> *All dressed up and no place to go.*
> *Jesus Called and Kim Answered.*
> *Now I know something you don't.*

Val McDermid, who became a writer against all odds, was asked for a six-word epigraph and chose *They Said I Couldn't Do It.* In Lorrie Moore's latest novel, *I Am Homeless if This is Not My Home,* there are two characters called Lily and Finn. Lily asks Finn if he would like a maudlin little quote on his headstone that sums up his life. He chooses *Well That Was Weird*. Lily doubts she'll have a headstone but thinks that *Peace, Y'all* might work.

Lucia Osborne-Crowley, in *I Choose Elena*, writes that she hoards things, clings to memories even when they have become so distant they feel like fantasies, and clings to fantasies as though they are memories. Sometimes she thinks that should be written on her tombstone.

What would you like as your epitaph? I used to think *She never had nor wanted a mobile phone* would be good, but then I caved and got one.

Here lies pencil woman was another thought.

My editor friend thinks he might like *Cool, calm, corrected*. Or here's a classic one for a writer: *Literally Dead*.

RITUALS

apple blossoms –
I walk the windy grounds
with a lit candle
– John F. Turner

As we age, ceremony and sacrament ritual can enrich our world, providing meaning, helping to combat gloom and ennui. Rituals can be everyday things: bowing to the sunset, praying at water's edge, saying grace at mealtimes. They may be things we've always done, or valuable additions to our treasure trove of things that bring solace. Ceremonial acts can be evoked at potent times, and included in the everyday fabric of our lives.

Many people find a silent morning routine an uplifting start to the day: prayer, meditation, journalling, gentle exercise such as yoga, tai chi, mindful walking or drinking the first cup of tea or coffee on the porch, listening to the birds. It might be an evening practice: lighting a candle in the garden and sitting quietly as dusk falls.

My granddaughters know several meal blessings. When they remember to say them and have decided which one to use, the family holds hands. Together they give thanks for the meal, and the myriad conditions that brought the food to them. Such sweetness, sharing moments of gratitude at the evening table.

Lighting a candle when we hear of a birth, a death, an illness or a tragedy is a simple ceremonial act which pays tribute to something important. It makes us feel better, that part is certain, and perhaps sends magic healing vibes into the cosmos, who can say.

Rituals can be borrowed or invented. I stole this one from a friend who chooses three words each morning as a foundation for the day. They set a positive intention, and are a way of responding, a beacon. She wouldn't tell me what hers were, but I bet they were lovely, because she is a person who radiates loveliness. I make up my own, changing them when I feel like it. *Relaxed, open* and *present* work for me. Or you can set a single word intention for your day, choosing a quality you want to practise, such as merriment, or gratitude.

Here is a ritual I invented. I collect the petals of dead roses and throw them in the air, while silently bestowing good wishes on someone who needs it, possibly me. My friends have a ritual for finding a parking spot. *Are you feeling lucky, very very lucky,* they sing in unison and hey presto, a parking space manifests. It usually works for them, and it doesn't hurt to try it.

You can use art and creativity in ritual ways, such as sewing a quilt to be buried in, or making a multimedia collage of your life, using paper, feathers, fabric scraps. You probably won't want to go as far as Arthur Bispo do Rosário, a Brazilian visionary who took fifty years to complete an ornately tasselled cloak which he planned to wear to meet God on the Day of Judgement.

In a long-lost book of ancient death rituals, I found an article about tear bottles. They were common in ancient Greece and Rome as well as in many Middle Eastern societies. It was once thought that mourners filled a small glass bottle or earthenware vessel with tears, to be placed in burial tombs or left at the beloved's grave as a sign of love and respect. Even if that tradition never actually existed, lachrymatory was 'revived' in Victorian times, and is still practised today. Tear bottles can also be gifted to the living, at a wedding or a birth. Any tiny bottle will do.

Other cultures have amazing rituals. Hatsumode is an auspicious Japanese tradition which began in the Edo period (1603–1868). It involves visiting a temple to pray for good fortune and protection on New Year's Eve. Shrines and temples open their gates to worshippers who wish to make their first prayers right at midnight. You can adopt a version of this by visiting a place of worship or a natural environment, offering thanks for your life, throwing fate into the winds as you farewell the old year and welcome the new one. Most of us have access to bushlands, public parks or the ocean, but a quiet moment under a tree or on a patio will do nicely.

Funerals are a good example of ritual. The traditional western funeral usually involves music, kind words, a slide show, tea, alcohol, and a decent spread. A current trend is for mourners to circle the coffin as a last farewell, quietly placing a flower or a rosemary twig in remembrance. Funeral practices in other places are highly varied, according to culture, religion and local custom. Hawaiian funerals involve chanting, the wearing of leis, and public oratory, when interesting and sometimes surprising things are said about the deceased. Then there is a feast of pork and greens cooked in coals, followed by canoeing out to sea and casting the ashes into the ocean.

Māori people conduct a tangi, or tangihanga, on the marae on the ancestral land of the deceased. The body rests in state for three days, with burial on the third. Relatives and friends come, sometimes from great distances, to address the gathering, offering blessings for the spiritual journey. Singing, joking and a free expression of grief is encouraged. It's traditional for mourners to wear wreaths of kawakawa leaves. Ritual prayers and cleansing incantations are made by the elders, and after the funeral there's a big night of song, dance and entertainment.

Every culture has its own way of disposing of bodies. Egyptians had intricate funerary rites, burying the dead with jewellery and artefacts made of gold and semiprecious stones for the wealthy; bone or glass for those of modest means. Tibetans traditionally cremate.

I mention the way other cultures do things because it provides a fluidity to our own ideas, encouraging us to think about the rituals we have or would like to adopt at our funeral or one we are organising. Learning about burial customs of other cultures invites us to contemplate the sort of funeral we'd like, and what rituals might be appropriate for us. You can choose Hindu chanting for your funeral, or mellow jazz, or Springsteen belting out.

The world is a big wide place with so many creative opportunities for us to enjoy ritual, both when we are alive and as we farewell the world in whatever way feels right to us. Peter Garrett says that traditional, dry, mournful rituals of farewell don't do lives much justice. At his send-off, he doesn't want breast-beating or self-pity. No howling at the moon. *Just put the music on and dance like there's no tomorrow.*

A LIST OF HELPFUL THINGS

It helps to not overthink everything.

It helps not to overthink anything.

It helps to trust the unknown moment.

It helps to breathe into your belly.

It helps to head your waka (canoe) in the right direction.

It helps to play with children, paint rocks and pretend you are a penguin.

It helps to relish the life you have, abandoning the fantasy of a better one.

It helps to have at least one item of clothing that makes you feel marvellous.

It helps to get out of town to see the starry night sky.

It helps to give, because you have plenty and some have not enough.

It helps to play Scrabble, especially when you get the Z.

It helps to understand that no feeling is final.

It helps to remember that everyone feels lost, ridiculous and sorrowful at times.

It helps to live merrily because when you're dead there won't be the opportunity. As my son Sam says, do not wait to carpe diem tomorrow.

TIME

There is no past and no future; no one has ever entered those imaginary kingdoms. There is only the present.
– Leo Tolstoy

Time seems to pass more quickly as we age, and we do not know why. Scientific and pseudoscientific theories abound but the mystery of time perception continues to elude us. One explanation is that our brains process less information as we grow older, which makes time seem to speed up. Time passes at the same rate as always, yet if you have ever sat at a meditation retreat, you will know that half an hour can be equivalent to four years, or ten minutes.

Anne Lamott speaks for many of us when she notes that one of the interesting aspects of getting old is how time races by. She suggests everything feels faster because it's going downhill, and it is unnerving.

Most of us have some version of this in our lives. How can it be time to clean the bathroom? I only did that yesterday, or was it two weeks ago? How did my tiny fairy granddaughter suddenly become a tall basketball-playing person? How did we get here so fast?

One of the things I like about being older is going slower. I have hurried all my life, and am still learning to be more leisurely in my approach to things. Not only are my days cruisier, but when the destination is the boneyard, why hasten.

Physics has a lot to say about time, much of it beyond the reach of a mortal with a normal-sized brain, but Einstein put it simply in a condolence letter just months before his own death. He pointed out that the distinction between past, present and future is a stubbornly persistent illusion, and that true reality is timeless.

What does this mean to us, in terms of living a wise life? If past and future are imaginary, we have only this moment in time, and we are part of a great spacious timelessness far bigger than our tiny selves. In a very literal sense, we have today, so let's use it well.

In the Tolstoy short story 'Three Questions', a king searches for answers to three important questions:

When is the most important time?
Who is the most important person to listen to?
What is the most important thing to do?

None of the answers given satisfy him, until finally an old hermit shows him that the most important time is now, the most important person is the one right in front of you, and the most important thing is to be kind.

We are older now, and possibly slightly wiser. We can enjoy creating realistic goals and we can be selective about how to spend our time and enjoy life to the maximum. Dr Bronwyn Herbert, a social worker and scholar in her nineties, recently completed her PhD on intergenerational homelessness, undeterred by being in hospital, caring for her husband or the death of her son. The late Lynn Ruth Miller became a standup comedian at age seventy. She was still going strong at eighty-six years old, living with a household of pets and buying herself flowers. Picasso and Matisse were producing great art in their final years.

We do not have to be these extraordinary people, but we can be encouraged by them. We can do astounding things, or choose to live simply and quietly, with composure, creativity, calm, contentment—despite climate change, world chaos and other people's craziness. We can savour it to the full, this precious, shitty, wonderful, puzzling life, so messy and mysterious. It contains jasmine incense, soft autumn light, a spicy meal, a woebegone friend, a dove outside the window. It contains our birth, our life, and our death. It gives us an opportunity to co-operate with change, to allow ebb and flow, delight, difficulty, shadow and moonlight. It makes sense to appreciate every moment of the time which remains to us.

MY DEAD FRIENDS—JOHN

long spring illness
sun faded overalls
on the line

in hospital –
knowing which day
by the food.

– John F. Turner

I'm walking down High Street Mall in Fremantle, past Culley's Tea Rooms.

You're not there, but your ghost is. This is the spot where I often ran into you, hanging about in your blue overalls, smoking rollies, ready for a chat. You liked to share a joke, or a poem, or a story. You went to India in your twenties, fried your brain on psychedelics, so the story goes, although schizophrenia might have been coming your way without the drugs. I met you at Zen. You couldn't meditate but you loved haiku and the teacher, so you used to turn up now and again. We became friends, sort of. Sometimes

I couldn't make head nor tail of you. When I shifted back to New Zealand, you'd ring at odd hours, deep in your illness. Once you rang at midnight to tell me to wear tinfoil on my head, because of Iraq.

When you became unwell you usually checked into hospital, and they looked after you until you were ready to face the world again. For years you were a heavy drinker—not a great combination with schizophrenia. When you got sober you were much happier. You were a serious haiku poet. Your work was very good.

Then cancer. I went to see you in palliative care. You were thin, but comfortable, wrapped in a colourful quilt, listening to the cricket. The orderly would wheel you outside so you could see the river and have a ciggie. You floated in and out of a morphine haze, ate the nectarine you'd asked me to bring. It was Christmas. You knew you were dying. You didn't seem fazed. You said something very wise about dying, which now unfortunately I have forgotten but it showed ease, a transcendence of the personal.

Once upon a time you had a beautiful love affair with a Japanese woman, or so the story goes.

You will always be there, ghost friend, outside Culley's in your overalls, ready for a yarn.

PARADOX

... do not grow old, no matter how long we live ...
never cease to stand like curious children before the great
Mystery into which we are born. – Albert Einstein

What an enigma this life is, so full of contradiction, inconsistency, absurdity, and impossibility.

Getting older is a time of great paradox, *n'est-ce pas*?

Some days I am contented, creative, and happy to be alive. I feel peaceful with the way things are, resigned to my body's limitations, at ease with my world as it is.

At other times, the reality of my ageing is daunting. I face hard days: the indignity of the loss of an ability, another friend in hospital, another funeral to attend. I am sad, frightened, world-weary, vulnerable, and very crotchety. Difficult feelings I have struggled with all my life are still with me, and now I face new situations, new strong feelings. Unpalatable emotions are normal, but they can seem unbearable.

The ability to hold opposite views in a gentle, accepting fashion is a sign of resilience and maturity, apparently. F. Scott Fitzgerald said that the test of a first-rate intelligence is the ability to hold two opposing ideas in mind at the same time while retaining the ability to function. He gives an example: we may see that things are hopeless yet be determined to make them otherwise. I am somewhat reassured by this.

It can be a hard call, however. Dealing with paradox makes us unhappy. It's an actual thing, known as cognitive dissonance, defined as the unpleasant emotions arising when two conflicting ideas cause emotional turmoil. It's an important field in social psychology.

Living with paradox is puzzling. You know a relationship, or a job, or an environment is not in your best interest. You say goodbye to it, then miss it desperately. You judge travelling friends for their fossil-fuel consumption in the same breath as looking up the airfare to Thailand. You enjoy the easy warm weather, while knowing there's been no rain for six months, which is ecologically bad news. You are conflicted in your close relationships to the point of dizzy confusion. You can love and need and value someone while also finding them batshit crazy and extremely annoying.

Jack Kornfield advised us to sit in the middle of it all, the paradox, the messiness, the hopes and the fears, not thinking that we have to fix it.

I recall (but not from where) that artist David Shrigley said something like *it's good and bad all wrapped up in the same brown paper bag*, and Buddhist monk Ajahn Brahm has a whole YouTube talk called 'Relax! Everything's Out of Control'. Anne Lamott's son, Sam, nailed it as a child when he told her he thought he had life figured out: *pretty good, some problems.* Many wise ones, all telling us the same thing.

I am learning to accommodate paradoxes, despite the complexities. I live in a world in which a billion children lack food, shelter, education, water and health services, and a bottle of whisky sells at Sotheby's for US$2.7 million. I live in a world that won't settle down and be sensible, but a difficult morning turns into an elegant afternoon all by itself.

Paradox is understanding that, as Jorge Luis Borges said, death is just infinity closing in. Also, the last plums of autumn taste wonderful and a clean bathroom brings a certain smug joy. One might as well embrace the messiness of being alive, the happiness of being older, and also the sadness. Fear and excitement, joy and sorrow, pleasure and pain: so closely linked sometimes one can't tell the difference.

If we can't find grace in this shifting world of ten thousand joys and ten thousand sorrows, then where can it be found?

It's an art, to recognise our blessings, to come to terms with the whole catastrophe of human existence, with all the parts that don't make sense and all the bits that do, with all our moments, surprising, alarming, splendid or dreadful. Things are the way they are, and they won't always go our way, and a lot of it just doesn't make sense—but it's all we've got. This very moment, this very life, in all its worn-out glory, its fabulous surprisingness—it's this and that, and abundant everything.

NOT TURNING AWAY

There are always flowers for those who want to see them.
– Henri Matisse

It's so hard to be brave sometimes. When your leg hurts so much that you can't walk properly, when two of your friends are in hospital, when just being alive, keeping the house clean and food in the cupboard feels exhausting and dreary.

It is hard not to turn away from the actuality of ageing, sickness and death.

Human beings can only bear so much reality, as T.S. Eliot said. We prefer our own version of things. We would like the whole shebang to be much more pleasing than it is, thank you very much. This applies to absolutely everything, including the ageing body, grumpy people, heatwaves, bad haircuts and dying bees.

I see this turning away in myself quite clearly.

For example, I like to be told I don't look my age. Flattering, yes, but it means I believe there is something wrong with looking my age. In the less intelligent part of my brain, I still cling to the religion of youth and beauty, which may be a crock but is a very culturally ingrained crock.

When I see someone decrepit, I don't immediately feel love and compassion. My first reaction can be a swampy blend of disgust, impatience and aversion. Is it them I am turning away from, or is it myself? For this is my fate too, unless I die soon, which I may but am not planning on.

Which brings me to the matter of the dying bee. Good, you may be saying, having wondered if I would return to the bees.

This morning, sweeping the patio, I found a bee in my dustpan. I waited for it to fly off, but it didn't. On closer inspection, I saw it was on its back, squirming and struggling, so I put it on the edge of the balcony and gently turned it up the right way. It continued writhing.

It was dying, I realised. I didn't want it to be dying and I didn't want to watch it dying. There is no real way to assist a dying bee. Squash it? That seemed cruel, and Buddhists are not meant to kill things. Maybe walk away and leave it to become a dead bee all by itself. Nothing felt right so I gave it a little push and it dropped down into the bush. This also felt wrong. A small incident, perhaps, but it seemed like a metaphor.

I wanted to turn away. We want to turn away. We want things to be better than they are. When things are just the way they are and we don't like it, we suffer. When we stick with the idea that things should be otherwise, we suffer.

Not only that, we also shut down.

In her poem 'Lead', Mary Oliver writes about watching loons dying on the beach, and how the death of precious life does not have to break your heart but rather can break your heart open. She is pointing us to see that being open-hearted means you are alive, and that you can respond to events, even hard ones, in a human way.

All the wise teachers talk about acceptance, but there is no magic bullet providing instant acceptance. If only we could buy a shitload and be done with it, but no, we must practise it. It takes insight and patience to learn acceptance. Be real about it. This is the way things are. The dying bee, the dying loons, your dying self.

Some people get mired in the *isn't it awful*s, which is the habit of whingeing and moaning about everything from the weather to the government to the price of groceries to the random smelly dude on the bus. There will always be something to complain about, and there will always be someone else to blame. The problem is that dwelling in the land of awful doesn't bring any happiness. Instead of dwelling on other people's awfulness, perhaps it is best not to be an awful person. The world does not devote itself to making us happy, so let us aim to be gracious and content whatever the circumstances.

My sister, who has lost two of her adult children, does

not complain. Despite her losses, she gets on with living. To celebrate turning eighty, she threw herself a birthday party, inviting old friends, new friends, residents and family to join her at her retirement village. There were Scrabble boards, a drawing table for the children, ice-cream with ginger sauce for all. Instead of dwelling in misery she offered kindness, fun and treats.

Recently I stooped to complaining about my neighbour, who has memory loss and some distressing habits. For a few months, I despised him. Grumble, grumble, grumble, mainly to myself but sometimes to others. At some point, because it was so unpleasant to be this way, my heart softened. I began to acknowledge his suffering and greeted him in a friendly manner. Now I enjoy our daily hello. I ask how he is. He replies *too early to tell*, and we laugh. I feel a lot better when I don't take the low road of meanness.

Knowing wise things and behaving wisely are different things but I take my own advice as often as I can. Recently I had a painful ear infection, and I foolishly added to my predicament with self-pity and being horrible to myself—not the best combination.

This is awful. I can't cope. How will my dying be gracious if I can't even cope with a sore ear? So easy to create extra trouble at no extra cost. Once I let go of my unhelpful thinking, things improved. I reassured myself that the antibiotics would soon kick in, and that when it's my turn to die I will manage it as best I can and that will be enough.

I ceased worrying about the bee, my writing deadline, and my uneven haircut, and went to the café for a soothing hot beverage, which I find to be a cure for almost everything.

ANOTHER LIST OF HELPFUL THINGS

Toast helps, so do teapots.

Dogs. Dusk. Jasmine. Mangoes.

Being with people who are funny, kind and interesting.

Saying no to things you don't want to do.

Sitting still and doing nothing. Watching how big that becomes.

Knowing that nothing is perfect, personal or permanent. The Buddha said that, but it took him more words.

It helps to be clear about what is our circus, which are our monkeys.

It helps to let things evolve at their own speed.

It helps to vow to save all beings, including ourselves.

It helps to be guided by this Tibetan aspiration: *In relating to the future of humanity, I will be optimistic and courageous.*

It can be useful to look in the mirror each morning and say 'Hello Beautiful', especially when you are feeling poorly.

ENDING

End and beginning are dreams.
– Bhagavad-gītā

Dinner over. A quiet interlude before bath and bed for the children. The sweet ordinary marvellousness of a cold winter evening. My son plays his guitar. Music unknown to me, delicate. Such a good man, some white in his beard now. My oldest granddaughter reads by the heater, deep in her dressing gown, deep in a book. The younger child dances to the music, twirling, wearing a special smile. *Look at me dancing. I am marvellous.* The joy of her, the joy of it, to lie on the sofa in my old-lady slippers, warm dog on my lap, tired and at peace, and yes, old. This poignant mixture of happiness and sadness so closely aligned I can't tell the difference. Savour, savour, for soon it will be gone, soon I will be gone.

May I be at peace with my life. May I bow to my moments as glad moments. May I live now, for I will never be this young again.

REFERENCES

Wherever possible, below, I have attributed quotes and ideas to their author and have sought permission for their use.

Allen, Neal. ('our only real job' and 'name our inner critic'), *Better Days: Tame Your Inner Critic*, Namaste Publishing, 2024.

Allen, Neal. ('volunteering at a hospice'), 'How I Got Here', *Shape of Truth*, shapesoftruth.com/neal-allen-bio.

Balan, Estelle, Anabelle Decottignies and Louise Deldicque. 'Physical Activity and Nutrition: Two Promising Strategies for Telomere Maintenance?', *Nutrients*, 7 December 2018, vol. 10, no. 12, article 1942, doi:10.3390/nu10121942. pmc.ncbi.nlm.nih.gov/articles/PMC6316700.

Blain, Georgia. *The Museum of Words: A Memoir of Language, Writing, and Mortality*, Scribe Publications, 2017.

Brach, Tara. *Radical Acceptance: Embracing Your Life with the Heart of a Buddha*, Bantam Books, 2003.

Bradshaw, Rebecca. *Rebecca Bradshaw's Dharma Talks*. dharmaseed.org/teacher/143.

Brahm, Ajahn. ('whole YouTube talk'), 'Relax! Everything's

Out of Control', 26 June 2015, youtube.com/watch?v=zY6Q-OnMTEE.

Brahm, Ajahn. ('young people'), ajahnbrahmpodcast.stream/episodes/a-buddhist-attitude-to-life-ajahn-brahm.

Camus, Albert. 'Return to Tipasa', *L'été: Les Essais LXVIII*, Gallimard, 1954.

Chiyo-ni. Quoted in Donegan, Patricia and Yoshie Ishibashi, *Chiyo-ni: Woman Haiku Master*, Tuttle Publishing, 1998.

Chödrön, Pema. ('lower your standards'), *When Things Fall Apart: Heart Advice for Difficult Times*, Shambhala, 2016.

Chödrön, Pema. ('no escape'), *The Wisdom of No Escape: and the Path of Loving-Kindness*, Shambhala, 2018.

Dass, Ram. ('his leg was old'), *Still Here: Embracing Aging, Changing and Dying*, Hodder Headline Australia, 2000.

Dass, Ram. ('take what comes'), *Grist for the Mill*, Harper Collins, 2014.

Dylan, Bob. 'I Shall Be Released', Capitol, 1968.

Einstein, Albert. ('reality is timeless'), letter to the family of Michele Besso, March 1955. Quoted in 'Some of Einstein's Reflections, Aphorisms and Observations', *The New York Times*, 29 March 1979.

Einstein, Albert. ('do not grow old'), letter to Otto Juliusburger, September 1947. Quoted in Dukas, Helen and Banesh Hoffmann (eds), *Albert Einstein, The*

Human Side: New Glimpses from His Archives, Princeton University Press, 1979.

Eliot, T.S. 'Burnt Norton', *Collected Poems, 1909–1935*, Harcourt, Brace and Company, 1958.

Emerson, Ralph Waldo. 'The American Scholar', speech given on 31 August 1837. Quoted in *American Transcendentalism Web*, Virginia Commonwealth University, archive.vcu.edu/english/engweb/transcendentalism/authors/emerson/essays/amscholar.html.

Enomoto, Eiichi. 'Hermit Crab'. Quoted in Shundo Aoyama, *Zen Seeds: 60 Essential Buddhist Teachings on Effort, Gratitude, and Happiness*, Shambhala, 2019.

Ferraro, Vinny. vinnyferraro.org.

Fitzgerald, F. Scott. 'The Crack-Up', *Esquire Classic*, 1 February 1936, classic.esquire.com/article/share/97a6b0a8-ba1c-4b7b-aa64-0d08dd9fb952.

Garrett, Peter. Interview by McMillen, Andrew, 'Peter Garrett on the Failure of the Voice Referendum, Protecting Cape York and Healing Old Wounds', *The Australian*, 9 March 2024.

Gibran, Kahlil. *The Prophet*, Alfred A. Knopf, 1923.

Goldsworthy, Peter. *The Cancer Finishing School: Lessons in Laughter, Love and Resilience*, Viking, 2024.

Hafeez, Kaamran and Al Batt. ('lost property') 'A Pair of Reading Glasses', *New Yorker*, 4 March 2024.

Han-shan. *Cold Mountain: 100 Poems by the T'ang Poet Han-shan*, trans. Burton Watson, Columbia University Press, 1970.

Herbert, Bronwyn. '90 year-old proves age is just a number, earning PhD', ABC Sydney, 23 December 2023, abc.net.au/listen/programs/sydney-mornings/age-is-just-a-number-90-year-old-earns-phd/103250848.

Hesse, Hermann. *Steppenwolf*, translated by Thomas Wayne, Algora Publishing, 2010.

James, Henry. *The Ambassadors*, Methuen, 1903.

Kabat-Zinn, Jon. *Full Catastrophe Living: How to Cope with Stress, Pain and Illness Using Mindfulness Meditation*, Piatkus, 1990.

Kafka, Franz. Quoted in Popova, Maria, 'Kafka on Books and What Reading Does for the Human Spirit', *The Marginalian*, themarginalian.org/2014/06/06/kafka-on-books-and-reading.

Kalanithi, Paul. *When Breath Becomes Air: What Makes Life Worth Living in the Face of Death*, Vintage Arrow, 2017.

Knaster, Mirka. 'Taking a Relaxed Approach with Sayadaw U Tejaniya', *Inquiring Mind*, vol. 24, no. 2, Spring 2008, inquiringmind.com/article/2402_18_knaster_takingarelaxedapproach.

Koren, Edward. 'The Decade of Wisdom', *New Yorker*, 5 February 2024.

Kornfield, Jack. *A Path with Heart: A Guide through the Perils and Promises of Spiritual Life*, Bantam, 1993.

Lamott, Anne. ('at 33, I knew everything'), 'At 33, I knew everything. At 69, I know something much more important', 21 November 2023, 3quarksdaily.com/3quarksdaily/2023/11/at-33-i-knew-everything-at-69-i-know-something-much-more-important.html.

Lamott, Anne. ('carbonated holiness'), interview by Rose, Daniel Asa, 'Radical Hope and Laughter: An Interview with Anne Lamott', *Literary Hub*, 9 November 2018, lithub.com/radical-hope-and-laughter-an-interview-with-anne-lamott.

Lamott, Anne. ('grandma pudding'), quoted in 'Postcards from the Rogue Valley', *Anne Lamott: Straight Talk on Aging, Miracles, Humor and More*, 4 February 2024, postcards-from-the-rogue-valley.blog/anne-lamott-straight-talk-on-ageing-miracles-humor-and-more.

Lamott, Anne. ('nailed it as a child'), *Travelling Mercies: Some Thoughts on Faith*, Anchor Books, 2000.

Lamott, Anne. ('one superpower'), 'A Superpower of Old Age: Powerlessness', *Washington Post*, 14 February 2024, washingtonpost.com/opinions/2024/02/14/friend-upset-do-nothing.

Lamott, Anne. ('time races by'), 'Age Makes the Miracles Easier to See', *Washington Post*, 17 January 2024.

Lowry, Brigid. *Juicy Writing: Inspiration and Techniques for Young Writers*, Allen & Unwin, 2008.

Lowry, Brigid. ('Yalgoo'), 'Yalgoo', *The Western Word*, vol. 19, no. 3, 1995.

Lowry, Brigid. ('you might as well laugh'), *With Lots of Love from Georgia*, Allen & Unwin, 2005.

Magnusson, Margareta. *The Gentle Art of Swedish Death Cleaning*, Simon & Schuster, 2017. (Show also available at SBS On Demand.)

Magnusson, Margareta. *The Swedish Art of Ageing Well*, Scribe, 2023.

Martin, Gary. 'Has the term "old" passed its retirement date?', *The West Australian*, 19 February 2024, thewest.com.au/opinion/gary-martin-has-the-term-old-passed-its-retirement-date-c-13615420.

Matisse, Henri. *Jazz*, Tériade, 1947.

McDermid, Val. 'My Secret Life: Val McDermid, 57, author', *Independent*, 24 October 2012, independent.co.uk/news/people/profiles/my-secret-life-val-mcdermid-57-author-8225178.html.

Moon, Susan. *This is Getting Old: Zen Thoughts on Aging with Humor and Dignity*, Shambhala, 2010.

Moore, Lorrie. *I Am Homeless if This Is Not My Home*, Faber Fiction, 2023.

Nuru, Ivan. @IvanNuru, X, 10 April 2018.

Oliver, Mary. 'Lead', *New and Selected Poems: Volume Two*, Beacon Press, 2007.

Osborne-Crowley, Lucia. *I Choose Elena*, Allen & Unwin, 2020.

Penick, Douglas J. *The Age of Waiting*, Arrowsmith Press, 2021.

Porter, Max. *Grief Is the Thing with Feathers*, Faber, 2016.

Radin, David. *A Temporary Affair: Talks on Awakening and Zen,* Monkfish Books, 2022.

Radnor, Josh. Interview by Rascoe, Ayesha, 'Joshua Radnor on his debut album and transitioning from TV to music', *Weekend Edition Sunday*, 17 December 2023, npr.org/2023/12/17/1219882811/joshua-radner-on-his-debut-album-and-transitioning-from-tv-to-music.

Richmond, Lewis, *Aging as Spiritual Practice: A Contemplative Guide to Growing Older and Wiser,* Penguin, 2012.

Roedel, John. ('every night'), Facebook, 20 February 2024, facebook.com/johnbigjohn/posts/every-night-before-i-go-to-sleepi-invite-all-of-my-beloveds-who-have-died-to-joi/10168160724255276/.

Sakaki, Nanao. *Let's Eat Stars*, Blackberry Books, 1997.

Seng-ts'an. Quoted in Weinstein, Warren Z., 'Translation by Richard B. Clarke of the *Hsin Hsin Ming* attributed to Seng Ts'an, the Third Chinese Patriarch of Zen', California

State University Long Beach, home.csulb.edu/~wweinste/HsinHsinMing.html.

Smith, Red. *To Absent Friends from Red Smith*, Atheneum, 1982.

Syme, Rodney. *A Completed Life*, Dying with Dignity Victoria, 2023.

Taylor, Cory. *Dying: A Memoir*, Text Publishing, 2016.

Tolstoy, Leo. 'Three Questions', *What Men Live By and Other Tales*, 1885. Translated by Aylmer and Louise Maude. Ebook published by Project Gutenberg, 2009, gutenberg.org/files/6157/6157-h/6157-h.htm#link2H_4_0014.

Turner, John F. *Observe the Changes: Haiku and Senryu*. A private collection given to friends.

Twain, Mark. *Mark Twain Speaking*, Paul Fatout (ed.), University of Iowa Press, 1976.

Vyasa, Krishna Dvaipayana. 'The Nature of Life and Death', *Bhagavad-gītā*, Chapter II—'Sankhya-Yog' ('The Book of Doctrines').

Yip-Williams, Julie. *The Unwinding of the Miracle: A Memoir of Life, Death and Everything That Comes After*, Random House, 2019.

FURTHER READING

Bayda, Ezra with Elizabeth Hamilton, *Aging for Beginners*, Wisdom Publications, 2018.

Bernhard, Toni. *How to Wake Up: A Buddhist-Inspired Guide to Navigating Joy and Sorrow*, Wisdom Publications, 2013.

Bolleter, Ross. *Dongshan's Five Ranks: Keys to Enlightenment*, Wisdom Publications, 2014.

Brett, Lily. *Old Seems to be Other People*, Hamish Hamilton, 2021.

Dass, Ram and Mirabai Bush. *Walking Each Other Home: Conversations on Loving and Dying*, Sounds True, 2018.

Doughty, Caitlin. *Smoke Gets in Your Eyes: And Other Lessons from the Crematory*, W. W. Norton & Company, 2014.

Fischer, Norman. *Training In Compassion: Zen Teachings on the Practice of Lojong*, Shambhala Publications, 2013.

Kenny, Rose Anne. *Age Proof: The New Science of Living a Longer and Healthier Life*, AWL, 2022.

Kornfield, Jack. All his many books.

Lowry, Brigid. *A Year of Loving Kindness to Myself & Other Essays*, Fremantle Press, 2021.

Narboe, Nan (ed.). *Aging: An Apprenticeship,* Red Notebook Press, 2017.
Rumi, Jelaluddin. *The Essential Rumi*, translated by Coleman Barks with John Moyne, Harper Collins, 1995.
Tolle, Eckhart. *Stillness Speaks,* Namaste Publishing and New World Library, 2003.

USEFUL ONLINE RESOURCES

Alzheimer's Association provides lots of information about what Alzheimer's does and doesn't look like. See alz.org.

CoGenerate. Their mission is to bring older and younger people together to solve problems, bridge divides and co-create the future. Visit cogenerate.org for more.

Granny Gets a Grip. Inclusive design for all ages—innovative and stylish products designed for ageing bodies can be found at grannygetsagrip.com.

Heart and Mind: The Website and Blog of Rabbi Johnathan Wittenberg. Jonathan Wittenberg is a philosopher, writer and Senior Rabbi of Masorti Judaism in the UK. See jonathanwittenberg.org.

Living Well, Dying Wise. facebook.com/dyingwise. Erin Griffing offers grief guidance, community education and end-of-life support to families and individuals.

mygriefassist.com.au/inspiration-resources is a brilliant website which provides a categorised list of movies themed around the human experience of loss and grief. It lists films to use as a resource if someone has lost a child, a parent or a sibling, amongst other losses. It also lists films about death to use with children of various ages, as well as many other useful grief-related issues.

Tender Funerals at tenderfunerals.com.au is a not-for-profit service that believes funerals should be authentic, affordable and meaningful, and encourages community and family participation.

If you are interested in **natural burials and DIY coffins,** here are some sites:

Adult Learning Australia has coffin-making classes: ala.asn.au/stories/diy-custom-made-coffins.

Leaving Lightly. Earth-friendly funeral products can be found at cardboardcoffinsaustralia.com.au.

Serendipity Coffins, is a Western Australian company selling caskets made of natural materials, including pandanus, banana leaves, bamboo, willow and wool. See serendipitycoffins.com.au.

ACKNOWLEDGEMENTS

Gratitude to Ro Cambridge, Vanna Lowry and my friend who is not really called Steve, for so generously contributing their thoughts and wisdom to this book.

Thanks to John Roedel and Ross Bolleter for permission to use their words and poems. Much gratitude to Irina Harford, Sally Gillespie, Perle Besserman and Mia Newman for their love, support and input to this book. A deep bow to the late John F. Turner. He shared his haiku so generously, and now I share them with you.

Warmest thanks to Sam Field for his idea of the Epitaph Game.

Palms together, with heartfelt gratitude, to all the dharma teachers who've guided me. I owe you everything. In particular: Ross Bolleter Roshi, Alexis Santos, Sayadaw U Tejaniya, Gil Fronsdal, Vinny Ferraro, Sharon Salzberg, Joseph Goldstein, and Jack Kornfield.

ABOUT THE AUTHOR

Brigid Lowry was born in New Zealand to a bohemian family where she learned to value books and writing. She hopes her work will inspire people to think, laugh and enjoy being alive. Brigid has an MA in Creative Writing and is the award-winning author of eight young adult titles, including the bestseller *Guitar Highway Rose*. Her recent titles are *Still Life with Teapot: On Zen, Writing and Creativity* (2016), and *A Year of Loving Kindness to Myself & Other Essays* (2021), both with Fremantle Press. She is in favour of kindness, vegetables and living simply.

ALSO BY BRIGID LOWRY

If you're struggling to maintain grace and good humour amidst daily potholes and pitfalls, Brigid Lowry may be just the warm, wise and witty companion you need. Informed by contemporary psychology and Buddhist philosophy, Brigid's essays offer reflections on everything from friendship to grief, and from gratitude to self-care. *A Year of Loving Kindness to Myself & Other Essays* is all the encouragement you'll need to nurture yourself and those around you.

'Brigid raises a brave teacup to the gnarly, mixed, yet ultimately generous provenance of this world. This artfully threaded string of honest, tender worry-beads—in the form of small unvarnished gems of hard-won self-acceptance—comes with far too much edgy candour ever to be mistaken for sticky "self-help". A tonic for the spirit. Recommended dosage: once daily, before sleep.'
—Susan Murphy, author of *Red Thread Zen*